THE ATHLETE'S BLUEPRINT TO SUCCESS

THE ATHLETE'S BLUEPRINT TO SUCCESS

ATHLETE HABITS, ATHLETE FINANCE, AND THE SCIENCE OF ATHLETIC PERFORMANCE EXPLAINED (3-IN-1 COLLECTION)

ATHLETE DOMINATION

HADLEY MANNINGS

Copyright © 2023 by Hadley Mannings

All rights reserved. No part of this book may be reproduced, stored in a retrieval system, or transmitted in any form or by any means, electronic, mechanical, photocopying, recording, or otherwise, without the prior written permission of the publisher, Book Bound Studios.

The information contained in this book is based on the author's personal experiences and research. While every effort has been made to ensure the accuracy of the information presented, the author and publisher cannot be held responsible for any errors or omissions.

This book is intended for general informational purposes only and is not a substitute for professional medical, legal, or financial advice. If you have specific questions about any medical, legal, or financial matters matters, you should consult with a qualified healthcare professional, attorney, or financial advisor.

Book Bound Studios is not affiliated with any product or vendor mentioned in this book. The views expressed in this book are those of the author and do not necessarily reflect the views of Book Bound Studios.

To all athletes who strive for excellence in their sport and life, this book is dedicated to you. May it serve as a guide to cultivate habits, manage finances, and understand the science of athletic performance to reach and maintain success. Keep pushing boundaries, never stop learning, and always believe in your potential.

"Success is not final, failure is not fatal: it is the courage to continue that counts."

— WINSTON CHURCHILL

CONTENTS

From the Author   xi
Introduction   xiii

ATHLETE HABITS

Introduction   3
1. Develop a Plan   7
2. Be Consistent and Focused   17
3. Visualization and Mental Training   29
4. Sleep, Rest, and Recover   45
5. Healthy Eating to Fuel Your Body   59
6. Improve Your Awareness   71
7. Build Your Network   83
8. Believe in Yourself   99
Epilogue   103

ATHLETE FINANCE

Introduction   109
1. Assets and Liabilities   113
2. Managing Cash Flow   113
3. Debt   125
4. Investments   147
5. Retirement Planning   169
6. Taxes   179
7. Legal Help, Athlete Image Entities, and Financial Advisors   187
Epilogue   195

THE SCIENCE OF ATHLETIC PERFORMANCE

Introduction	199
1. Anatomy and Physiology of Athletic Performance	201
2. Genetics and Athletic Performance	209
3. Training for Athletic Performance	215
4. Nutrition and Athletic Performance	223
5. Performance-Enhancing Substances and Doping	229
6. Psychological Factors in Athletic Performance	237
7. Recovery and Injury Prevention in Athletic Performance	243
8. Technology and Athletic Performance	249
9. Environmental Factors in Athletic Performance	255
Epilogue	263
Afterword	265
About the Author	267
From the Author	269

~~$10.99~~ FREE EBOOK

Receive Your Free Copy of Legends of the Game

Or visit:
bookboundstudios.wixsite.com/hadley-mannings

INTRODUCTION

Athletics is a highly competitive and demanding field where success is the result of a combination of physical and mental prowess, sound financial planning and management, and an understanding of the science behind athletic performance. As a result, athletes and coaches have always searched for the secrets to peak performance. This comprehensive guidebook, *"The Athlete's Blueprint to Success,"* provides a roadmap to athletic success. This 3-in-1 collection encompasses all aspects of athletic success, from developing winning habits and routines to managing finances and understanding the science of athletic performance.

In this comprehensive guidebook, you'll learn about the importance of setting achievable goals and developing a healthy routine and the financial literacy and management skills crucial to securing a successful future as an athlete. The book also offers a deep dive into the anatomy and physiology, training principles, nutrition, psychology, and technology that contribute to athletic performance. Understanding these factors is crucial to optimizing physical and mental performance and achieving your goals as an athlete.

Whether you're an aspiring athlete looking to take your performance to the next level or a seasoned coach looking to help your

Introduction

athletes reach their full potential, "*The Athlete's Blueprint to Success*" provides a comprehensive guide to success in athletics. The book has been crafted to provide a clear, concise, and actionable guide to success in the field. In addition, it has been designed to help athletes and coaches achieve their full potential. So, whether you're a seasoned pro or just starting, "*The Athlete's Blueprint to Success*" provides the roadmap you need to reach the pinnacle of success in athletics.

ATHLETE HABITS

8 FUNDAMENTAL HABITS THAT ELITE ATHLETES CULTIVATE TO REACH AND MAINTAIN SUCCESS

INTRODUCTION

CITIUS - ALTIUS - FORTIUS

— THE OLYMPIC
MOTTO

These Latin words translate to "faster - higher - stronger."

You don't have to be an Olympic athlete to want to become faster and stronger. You don't need to be an Olympic athlete to want to perform better in your sport. You certainly don't have to be an Olympic athlete to learn from other Olympic and professional athletes and borrow some of their training techniques.

Different athletes have different habits, and different practices have varying degrees of success for different people.

The greatest sprinter of all time, Jamaica's Usain Bolt, certainly has habits that have propelled him to greatness. His swagger and comedic antics at the starting line work for him.

Michael Phelps also has highly effective habits, but his approach to beginning a race looks very different from Bolt's. He sits down. He listens to music and has a much more cerebral and contemplative approach.

Introduction

It doesn't matter which athlete you identify with or your current level of athletic performance—learning about the best of the best and what makes them that way will open up pathways to improve yourself.

Who is this book for?

If you want to be on top of your game every day, this book is for you.

If you are frustrated by spending time and effort searching for answers and information to help your athletic development, this book is for you.

If you want to see beyond the trendy diets, gimmicks, and the trendy fads in working out, this book is for you.

If you don't want one approach pushed upon you, but would rather have several options that are tested and vetted by professional athletes presented to you—so that you can choose which is best for you—this book is for you.

This book is for athletes with significant levels of experience, upcoming young athletes who have lots of potentials, people who want to take their local game to the next level, or are people who are just getting started.

Coaches and trainers will find cutting edge insight into methods and effective habits for optimizing sports performance.

For those athletes, coaches, and trainers who have been focusing primarily on physical training, this book might open your mind to the authentic power of mental training for athletes.

According to the science behind the practice of yoga, the body only executes activities. The activities all originate inside the athlete's mind.

When athletes compete, the split-second decisions and responses to external activity are critical. The most complex piece of athletic performance is the correct identification of signals and the selection, production, and on-the-spot improvisation of accurate responses.

Think about how complex that is. These things don't just happen.

The development of healthy mental habits allows the athlete's mind to access memories and hopes for the future to enable the correct response to emerge.

Athletes who tap into the power of mental training take advantage of this competitive edge.

Unfortunately, athletes that only focus on the physical aspects of training do not have access to this untapped potential.

What is this book about?

Athletes need to have the mindset of a warrior to succeed. All human beings need to excel, but athletes are different.

Athletic competition is born from this need. Throughout history, warriors fought and battled against one another to prove their superiority. As civilization advanced, the need for this competition and battle emerged in the form of competitive sports. However, the need to compete behind the struggle and the pride of victory remains the same.

Due to this link between sports and battle, competition and the need to emerge victoriously relate to killer instincts. Focus, split-second decision making, and precise execution are all required in war and, of course, in athletics. To achieve this kind of performance requires self-control of thoughts, emotions, behaviors, and habits.

In sports, we all know that the better player does not always win—the player who plays better wins.

Athletes who consistently win can never sit back and relax. Just because they have always won or usually win does not mean they will continue to win.

The opposite is also true. Teams that consistently lose will not lose forever.

Athletes that understand the eight fundamentals habits required to improve have a genuine chance of becoming champions.

Although winners and losers are often determined mainly by physical prowess, everyday habits and training of the mind can ignite personal athletic growth.

This book proves that adopting habits used by other successful athletes is critical for every aspiring athlete who wants to improve their game. You'll find many examples of top athletes who use these habits, so you know they have **credibility**.

Introduction

What can people take away from this book?

When you finish reading this book, you will have learned practical steps that are realistic for anyone to take to adopt and benefit from these eight habits.

You will learn simple, meaningful, and practical strategies and habits to develop athletic performance. Whether you are looking to run faster, jump higher, throw farther, or improve your overall approach to your sport and yourself as an athlete, this book is for you.

When athletes train and compete without a roadmap, they leave the potential for great achievement on the table. Great athletes research best practices and follow the advice from athletic thought leaders to achieve continuous progress in their field.

With this book and the habits within, you will walk away with a roadmap that will lead you to results you may never have thought you could have achieved.

With practice, persistence, and commitment, you will achieve results.

1

DEVELOP A PLAN

Developing a plan helps athletes improve their capacity to focus their energy. Focusing on planning and goals helps athletes develop habits that govern emotions, thought processes, and actions.

Goals might involve developing and cultivating better habits or breaking harmful and unwanted habits.

Designing goals that boost motivation is critical for improvement. Athletes should ask themselves what it is that truly motivates them to want to set goals and achieve outcomes. Doing so reinforces an athlete's commitment and taps into the inner drive that sustains the athlete through the bad times and the good.

Athletes need the will to face hardships and endure the challenges that lie ahead. They need the discipline to build stamina and avoid distractions. Being powered and fueled by clearly identified inner desires will enable athletes to plan and set appropriately challenging and achievable goals.

What Is Goal Setting for Athletes?

When Michael Phelps was eight years old, he wrote a list of goals. The goal that topped the list was Phelps' dream to make the Olympics. Well, we all know how that turned out.

His goals don't stop there. Throughout his career, Phelps also set goals for his season. For each racing event, he set smaller short-term goals for the beginning, middle, and end of his season.

Research shows that when we take the extra few minutes to write down our goals, we increase our chances of achieving success by 33% (Price-Mitchell, 2018).

Goal setting is the process of leveraging your core values about success in your particular sport to evaluate your performance and achieve your personal best.

How Should Athletes Set Goals?

For many years, people have used the acronym SMART to set goals in all areas of life, from personal and professional to educational and athletic goals.

The acronym stands for Specific, Measurable, Attainable, Relevant, and Time-Bound. When it comes to athletic performance, here are what SMART goals look like for athletes:

Specific – Professional athletes and their trainers use specific goals, and so should you. Specific goals enable athletes to hold themselves accountable. You can't say if you're pitching more accurately, but you can tell if you are throwing first-pitch strikes with more frequency.

A simple formula to ensure the goal is specific enough: I will [state goal] by [doing what? How often? When?].

Measurable – When goals are measurable, athletes can quantifiably evaluate progress toward reaching those goals. If Michael Phelps' time on the breaststroke weren't progressing in the middle of his season towards the goal he set, it would alert him that something wasn't working. He could then redirect his training regimen or make other adjustments.

Attainable – Goals, of course, should be sufficiently challenging and above your current level of play and performance. They should push you from your comfort zone and require a real commitment. At the same time, goals should be attainable. Attainable goals are possible to achieve. Unrealistic setting goals can cause confidence setbacks, which are good for no one. Work with a growth mindset that seeks to move the needle. If you are someone who makes free shots 40% of the time, a 55% goal is more realistic than a 75% goal. You can always adjust the goal to make it more challenging along the way. Wouldn't that feel great?

Relevant – A relevant goal aims to take you from where you are to where you want to go. Objective assessments of gap analysis drive relevant goals. This assessment should be a combination of self-assessment and feedback from coaches and data. Motivational speakers like Tony Robbins have been wildly successful at encouraging goal setting because they understand people and what makes them tick. One strategy that Tony Robbins encourages others to adopt is what he calls the "pull strategy." Besides focusing on what you have to do, Robbins recommends reframing that behavior to become motivated by what you want to do. For example, going out for a run is a push strategy because it's part of your regular workout routine. Pull strategy reframes that run to propel you toward a meaningful goal of scoring more runs for your team. Robbins says, "The person who is motivated by necessity is interested in what's known and what's secure. The person who is motivated by possibility is equally interested in what's not known. He wants to know what can evolve, what opportunities might develop" (Ward, n.d.).

Time-bound – Adding a timeline for accomplishing milestones and goals increase the likelihood that you will stay on track and achieve your goals. An approaching deadline helps athletes maintain the self-discipline required to do whatever it takes to achieve that goal. For example, athletes might complete early morning training sessions or skip social activities to get in additional practice.

Below are a few examples of goals developed using the **SMART** framework:

By the first day of gameplay, [TIME-BOUND]
I will throw first-pitch strikes [SPECIFIC]
to eight of ten batters [MEASUREABLE].

The wording in the goal won't necessarily tell us if the goal is ATTAINABLE or RELEVANT. To ensure that your goals meet these criteria, try to be introspective, and consult with a coach to ensure the goals are appropriately set.

Why Do Athletes Set Goals?

A national championship field hockey coach strongly believed that a successful goal-scoring play must include **ten successful passes** before the shot on goal is taken. The coach put more emphasis on the passing game than on the goal itself.

The game transformed quickly. Players quickly adjusted their position to get themselves open and ready to receive the ball. The player in possession focused on passing and getting into a position to receive again. The coach loudly counted the passes to encourage the team. With each pass, the team remained focused on the passing game and never favored any particular player to score a quick goal.

Did they regularly pass ten times? No. In fact, at first, their scoring numbers decreased.

However, as the team gelled under this strategy, they gained momentum, scoring more, and ultimately winning the national championship. Wins were satisfying for every player.

Ten passes' short-term goal provided a laser-specific strategy that created focus and enthusiasm among the team and each player.

Goal setting provides many benefits for athletes:

Sustains Motivation and Focus

Athletes should use historical data to design attainable short-term goals that align with long-term goals. These short-term goals will motivate athletes to continue their pursuit of long-term goals. When this happens, the athlete is likely to sustain and even increase their focus and train even harder.

Improves Performance

Athletes who are driven by goals are more likely to concentrate on the task at hand. The focus is on the process rather than the outcome.

Some athletes use goals to focus on the here-and-now of their training. For example, a runner might repeat a mantra associated with the goal. A cyclist might focus on smooth and efficient pedaling by imagining the wheels of a steam train.

When athletes focus on goals and the process associated with achieving them, they can ignore the outcome, which can be overwhelming and instead concentrate specifically on the task.

When athletes dedicate their attention to the present moment, that attention tends to be quite powerful. This focus can significantly increase the likelihood of achieving that process goal.

Provides a Calming Effect

Past mistakes and failures tend to creep into the memory and cause the same errors to occur repeatedly—this may lead to a fear of the future. Fretting over the past and fearing the future are two unwanted behaviors that must be incorporated when athletes consider goal planning.

Creating a goal to focus on excellence and honoring it will reduce these two unwanted behaviors. It will also provide a calming effect. A goal like this can trigger you to produce excellence whenever you see it.

Knowing that a plan is in place to manage overall athletic performance leads to decreased stress and anxiety in the mind of the athlete. Goals can be soothing reminders that assist in achieving the desired outcome.

The athlete can relax at the end of the day, knowing that everything that they could have done has been done to achieve the best possible outcome. Without well-designed goals, the question of "What if?" can cause unnecessary stress during less-than-perfect practice and competition.

Encourages Self-Improvement

Setting goals results in improved athletic performance, but the byproducts of setting, measuring, and achieving goals is immensely valuable. Athletes benefit from the boost in self-confidence that comes from achieving goals. Also, focusing on personal goals nurtures the positive habits that focus on the athlete rather than comparing the athlete to others.

Impacts Perception About the Future

When athletes set goals, they are tapping into their ability to affect their future positively. Setting and achieving goals helps the athlete remember that they do have control over their performance. This feeling is called an internal locus of control. Studies show that people with an internal locus of control believe that their actions and skills determine success, and they have more positive feelings about how their efforts impact the outcome.

How Should Athletes Set Goals?

Imagine a mountain climber who has a long-term goal of completing a climb. Strategically designed short-term goals are crucial to achieving the long-term goal.

When setting goals, today's practice should be considered just as important as the ultimate competition. Giving equal weight to short-term and long-term goals is critical.

Short-Term Goals

Short-term goals are those that can be achieved within a short period and provide immediate feedback.

Short-term goals can help athletes remain grounded and focused as they endure the moment-to-moment struggles involved with intense training and competition.

Rather than focusing on uncontrollable factors like the score or the overall team performance, short-term goals refocus the athlete's attention to items over which they do have control. When athletes identify elements over which they have power and use those elements to design short-term goals, they can concentrate on energy, which can significantly influence the result.

Athletes can use short-term goals in a single session or a series of sessions. Short-term goals help to maintain forward momentum and establish the foundation for achieving long-term goals. Short-term goals should include actionable and measurable milestones that align with long-term goals.

Considering that achievement is motivational, short-term goals provide athletes with a sense of accomplishment that conditions the mind to see goals as challenges instead of obstacles.

Following a few simple steps will make establishing short-term goals easy and attainable.

Begin with the end in mind. Begin with the end goal in mind, continue to work backward, and drill it down to be as specific as possible in the short-term. If a baseball player who is currently batting .280 has a long-term goal to bat .300 by the end of the season, that player should work backward and begin by asking "What would it take for me to achieve this long-term goal?" Finding the answer will lead to the right short-term goals. More batting practice is good. Fifteen minutes per day of additional batting practice is better. Drilling down all the way, however, will result in a better outcome. For example, if data shows the player has trouble hitting the curveball, a short-term goal should be designed to address that particular pain point.

Be specific. No item is too specific. Goals surrounding analytics, work ethic, rest, attitude, prompt attendance, and performance during warm-ups can be meaningful if appropriately designed. A short-term goal for the baseball player in the above example may be to obtain data from coaching staff and spend an hour per week analyzing areas for improvement.

Use positive phrasing. When designing goals, positively phrased goals are more motivational than negatively phrased goals. For example, a negative goal like "commit fewer fouls" can be rephrased as "complete five foul-free minutes of scrimmage play." Athletes can then focus on achieving success rather than eliminating failure.

Examples of short-term goals include:

- Increase weights by 5% every week.
- Practice free throws for 20 minutes five times per week.
- Spend an additional 10 minutes in the cages per practice hitting curveballs.

Long-Term Goals

Long-term goals are the driving force behind why you play, compete, practice, and participate in your sport. Most people underestimate what they can achieve in the long term.

There are a few different types of goals. It's important to understand the different types as you design your long-term goals since different types have different degrees of success and affect athletes and their performance.

Outcome goals - Outcome goals refer to winning and losing. Athletes have little control over these goals.

Performance goals - Performance goals refer to independent athlete performance as it applies to their standards for excellence. Here, athletes have much more control as this type of goal only measures their performance.

Process goals - Process goals refer to the proficiency an athlete demonstrates in performing a particular skill, technique, or strategy. For example, in basketball free throws, the skill might be achieving an arc on the throw. In baseball, the batting skill might be keeping the player's head still while swinging the bat.

All of these goals are important in developing an athlete's overall skills. Still, studies show that athletes who concentrate on process and performance goals benefit from the process of goal setting more than those who focus on outcome goals. These athletes also reported better athletic performance, felt more confident, focused, and satisfied, and were less anxious.

Make no mistake. As athletes work towards long-term goals, there will be failure along the way.

Yankees legend Derek Jeter often says that the path to success isn't always about winning. Jeter said one of the best qualities about coach Joe Torre was his calm and supportive demeanor. Believe it or not, Jeter made mistakes. Torre encouraged him to keep swinging for the fences instead of becoming too cautious.

Jeter always respected Torre for allowing him to fail because it also allowed him to succeed.

The Goals Are Established. Now What?

Once short and long-term goals have been properly established, the process is long from over. If goals are used effectively, they are used as part of an ongoing process that includes the following steps:

Reevaluation

Depending on the situation, athletes should review the progress made to maintain focus and sustain momentum. Although still effective if done independently, athletes should perform this evaluation with a coach, mentor, or teammate.

Perhaps goal difficulty was miscalculated, and athletes need to adjust goals that were too easily achieved or too challenging.

Progress recognition and encouragement

Again, even if the athlete performs this exercise independently, it can be very effective. An athlete can reward themselves with a massage or a new piece of training equipment once milestones are achieved.

Coaches who publicly or privately recognize athletes as they progress toward goals provide motivation.

Acknowledge and evaluate obstacles

For many athletes, obstacles will arise during the pursuit of long-term goals. Whether athletes experience a physical plateau, a lack of confidence, or problems balancing other commitments, the key is to identify and acknowledge these obstacles and develop strategies to deal with them.

Goal progress feedback and evaluation

Having some level of accountability to an external source seems to be effective in maintaining confidence and motivation.

Research found that when external feedback is added to the goal achievement process, significantly higher performance - 17% higher - was the result.

Points to Remember

- Developing a plan helps athletes develop the capacity to focus their energies.
- Taking the extra few minutes to write down goals increases the chances of achieving success.
- Goals should be SMART: Specific, Measurable, Attainable, Relevant, and Time-Bound.
- Giving equal weight to short-term and long-term goals is critical.
- For goals to be used effectively, they must be used and reevaluated as part of an ongoing process.

2

BE CONSISTENT AND FOCUSED

Consistency

Everyone is after the ideal performance state. The self-improvement industry exists because of this elusive desire.

Athletes are no different.

When athletes are in the ideal performance state, they feel mentally and physically focused and confident that they will perform at a level of personal excellence.

Talk to athletes. They will tell you that when they have performed particularly well, they have been confident, focused, and completely immersed in the present moment. It's that feeling of 'flow' when every piece of the puzzle fits perfectly in place.

To achieve flow during a competition, athletes must do everything to put themselves on 'autopilot' by trusting their practice and training to take over. For this to happen, consistency must be utilized when developing a training regimen.

Most athletes have heard about the importance of being consistent. But the concept can often be too vague to be meaningful. When athletes think about consistency, they might wonder:

- What exactly does that mean?
- Do all repetitive behaviors count? Aren't some just superstitious?
- What behaviors should I be considering?
- Will it make a difference in my athletic performance?

Research about consistency reports on closed skills such as a golf putt, a baseball swing, or a basketball free throw. The bottom line is that athletes who utilize strategies that reinforce consistency enjoy improved performance.

Recycling

For athletes and everyone else, one thing is for sure. Everybody makes mistakes.

However, when athletes make a mistake in competition, it is critically important to let it go immediately. These skills can be learned and practiced to ensure they are consistently applied.

When an athlete is not performing well and becomes frustrated, the wheels fall off, making it very difficult to recover. However, athletes that find themselves not performing well can draw upon consistent strategies to pull themselves back up to avoid frustration. They may find their way to a very different outcome.

Athletes should examine their performance to identify the most common situations where they encounter difficulty and practice working through such situations during training exercises. Practicing these coping skills will develop positive habits that will result in positive reactions to mistakes and poor overall levels of play. When the athlete learns these recycling skills during training, they can transfer them to perform during competition.

Athletes who have not consistently practiced recycling skills during practice are likely to overcompensate for mistakes or poor performance and get into even deeper trouble.

An athlete who consistently lets go of a mistake returns immediately to the task at hand and maintains confidence and composure will have an exponentially greater result than one who does not.

Simulation Training

Simulation training sometimes called adversity training, is a strategy that replicates key elements of competition, which can often be adversarial. For example, football, soccer, or rugby teams will simulate stadium noise in advance of a, particularly competitive match. Practicing amid such conditions prepares athletes to face the conditions in real-time and maintain concentration.

Research suggests that an athlete's recall of information is facilitated by conditions that look, sound, and feel like those where the original training took place. Two primary benefits will often result from simulation training.

- **Positive transfer benefits.** When athletes replicate the environment they expect to compete in during their practice, they can expect to enjoy positive transfer benefits.
- **Improved concentration.** Another advantage of simulation training is its tendency to help athletes maintain focus and decrease the likelihood that unexpected events will distract during competition.

A famous example of simulation training involves Michael Phelps. His coach, Bob Bowman, was infamous for confiscating or breaking Phelps' goggles during practice to train Phelps to maintain concentration without clear goggles. Believe it or not, Phelps' goggles broke during an event in the 2008 Olympics. For the last 100 meters of the race, Phelps swam with broken goggles and won the gold medal.

Pre Performance Routines

Athletics are heavily ritualized. Successful athletes have realized that consistently engaging in preparatory rituals promote excellent performance.

- A player about to shoot a foul shot or serve a tennis ball bounces the ball a certain number of times.
- A softball or baseball player takes three practice swings and might touch the plate before getting into a ready position.
- A golfer might ensure the tag writing on their ball is lined up with the hole before taking a putt.

These rituals are called pre-performance routines. Athletes typically perform such routines just before competing in a self-paced activity that happens independently at the athlete's pace and without external interference.

Pre-performance routines improve concentration because they enable athletes to:

- Remain laser-focused in the present moment. The sequential and repetitive nature of a routine requires concentration to quiet thoughts about past performance or future outcomes.
- Pay complete attention to a specific action over which they have significant control. By paying attention to task-relevant information, the distraction of other irrelevant stimuli can be minimized.
- Ignore - and even block out - otherwise distracting external activity and thoughts. Paying total attention to one step of a routine after another requires the athlete to focus the entirety of their mental effort. In doing so, appropriate subconscious thoughts can arise in stressful situations to suppress negative thoughts.

Although these pre-performance routines provide a substantial improvement in intentional and attentional behavior, they are sometimes viewed as superstitious. However, it is important to differentiate between pre-performance routines and superstitious behavior.

A tennis player who needs their water jug in the same place on the court and facing in a certain direction before a match is not employing pre-performance routines, they are employing superstition. This qualifies as superstitious behavior since this activity is not logically or rationally causal in the athlete's performance outcome.

Pre-performance routines can be proven to influence the outcome because they enable the athlete to exert control over preparation, skill, strength, focus, etc.

The individual characteristics of the athlete should drive the structure and composition of the routine. For example:

- Stage of learning and experience
- Skill level
- Mental and physical characteristics
- Coping resources
- Situational variables

Also important in designing a pre-performance routine is the desired task-specific performance outcome. There should be a clear relationship between the pre-performance routine and its functionality. For example, if a golfer is incorporating the process of looking at the flag before a tee shot, there should be a specific reason behind such behavior. Perhaps the golfer is working on the task-specific goal of a more accurately directed shot.

Pre-performance rituals that generate peak performance have these characteristics:

- They are consistent. Research shows that elite golfers do the same thing in the same order with the same timing.
- They are used regardless of the situation. Whether trailing or leading by a large differential or a small one, research shows that elite golfers who never fail to practice their routine – every single time in every situation - gain an edge

over highly competent golfers who practice their routine less consistently.
- They are planned for specific situations. Situation specific stress, when anticipated, can be overcome with a pre-performance ritual. Efforts should be concentrated on reducing the tensions that can manifest during competition.

Motivation

One area that is particularly hard to remain consistent in is motivation. Consistent and repetitive training can't happen without motivation.

Athletes and trainers can optimize motivation with the following suggestions.

Be aware of motivation drains. Particularly tough physical, mental, and emotional training sessions can threaten to decrease motivation significantly. The same is true for poor performance during competition or even excellent performance. This resulted in a loss because of an external circumstance like a bad call by an official.

Sustain motivation mid-season. It's natural for motivation to be high at the start of a season and wane as the season goes on. If properly designed and executed, goal setting should pay attention to maintaining motivation and include steps for doing so.

When Things Go Wrong

Maintaining consistency when up against a formidable opponent or while losing is everything.

What happens when things go wrong?

During the 2012 Olympic soccer finals in London, Mexico was up against the team expected to win, Brazil. Brazil was the reigning Olympic soccer champion. On paper, they were by far the best team.

Mexico, on the other hand, was not expected to put up much of a fight. But they did.

Mexico went to Brazil in an incredible display in the finals. Brazil's players lost their composure. Fans watched in shock as the Brazil players hung their heads. They had not expected things to go this way.

Mexico ended up winning.

Maintaining consistency and avoiding overconfidence requires planning and even practice.

Focus

- What does it mean to focus?
- What benefits come from focusing?
- How do elite athletes stay extremely focused?

Imagine the focus a soccer goalkeeper must maintain to protect the goal during the opposing team's corner kick. The goalkeeper must maintain laser-focused on the incoming ball's flight path and tune out multiple distractions, including the movement of the players, noise, doubts, etc.

How can athletes focus on the most important components of practice and competition while at the same time blocking out internal and external distractions?

The answer is focus. When we focus, we exert mental energy to concentrate only on the external events happening around us and internal thoughts in our minds that are productive in accomplishing specific goals for successful athletic performance.

Poor performance often results from a small mistake. In many cases, that small mistake can be attributed to a lack of focus. The good news is that with dedication and practice, athletes can easily develop and strengthen their ability to focus.

Researchers acknowledge the importance of maintaining focus and have been studying it for years. Sports psychologists have studied strategies that improve athletic focus. Different strategies have different rates of success, depending on the sport and the athlete, of course. Still, they all aim to support a state of mind that is focused on peak performance.

Recognize When You're Getting In Your Own Way

Being able to focus is one thing. Focusing in the right way and on the right things is another.

When athletes focus on themselves and their performance too intensely or for too long, they can experience analysis paralysis. Being able to recognize when this, or any problem associated with maintaining focus, is happening is an important first step to rectifying it.

Human beings are motivated by one of two things in everything they do. They either try to achieve pleasure or avoid pain.

Believe it or not, athletes are sometimes afraid to succeed. Your brain can sometimes subconsciously link pain with success.

Why would the brain do such a thing?

The human brain does not work logically. It works based on association. If you've never been successful in your sport, success is an unknown factor. The brain understands the status quo. The status quo makes the brain feel comfortable. In contrast, the brain also often associates the unknown with pain.

Make sure to check yourself and ensure that your brain is not self-sabotaging.

How can you do this?

- Condition your brain to expect success.
- Develop beliefs that you are capable and worthy of success.
- Know that you already have everything you need to become successful. Train your mind to know it's there for the taking.
- Recognize the abundant nature of the resources available to you since lack attracts lack and abundance attracts abundance.
- Try to acknowledge that we are all equal in our opportunities, but where we differ is decision making, education, motivation, empowering beliefs, and how much we demand from each other and ourselves.

Set Performance Goals

We discussed the importance of goal setting in the previous chapter. Research that identifies successful strategies for maintaining an athlete's focus reinforces the importance of goal setting.

Here, understanding the different types of goals that exist is important:

- Outcome goals are about winning and losing and often involve a variety of factors outside of the athlete's control.
- Performance goals are focused on tasks relevant to the athlete's performance and are, therefore, within the athlete's control.

As one might imagine, research proves that athletes who focus on performance goals like increasing the first-pitch strike percentage or playing longer periods of foul-free basketball achieve greater focus. Athletes who focus on outcome goals like striking out more batters or winning the game are less likely to achieve focus-related success.

The increased concentration ability for athletes who focus on performance goals is likely to result from fewer external distractions. In the above example, the pitcher who focuses on the performance goal of throwing more first-pitch strikes is concentrating solely on their controllable task-relevant performance. In contrast, a pitcher who focuses on the outcome goal of striking out more batters is likely to be distracted by external variables like the batter's statistics, place in the batting order or performance of their last bat.

Positive Self-Talk

To maintain focus as they train and compete, many athletes talk to themselves.

Yes, they talk to themselves.

They remind themselves, silently, about their ability, their preparedness, certain skills they want to employ, etc. Others talk to themselves less positively.

How athletes talk to themselves is so important.

The problem is that for human beings, the default setting is to rely upon habitual vocabulary or the vocabulary that exists beneath our consciousness. When athletes experience stress or other negative emotions, they have the human tendency to draw from that habitual vocabulary. For many people, the habitual vocabulary can be quite negative.

The words we think and speak become our experience. Words have a biochemical effect on the body. For example, when an athlete uses a phrase like "we got crushed" in a negative way, they will produce very different biochemical effects than if they were to say, "We lost, but we know what to work on."

Human beings have needs that must be met. Athletes have those same needs. One need is to feel safe and supported. The inner voice of an athlete has more power than many realize.

We use words to interact with others daily, but the words we choose to speak and think can have a significant impact on how we feel, behave, train, and perform.

Try this:

- Change just one keyword in your vocabulary by removing a negative one or including a new word that inspires you.
- Aim to use this new word once a day verbally, once a day in your journal, and many times a day in your thoughts about the training and competing.

Through this simple activity, athletes can begin to change their routine vocabulary and self-talk habits to change how they think, feel, and perform drastically.

Transforming your vocabulary accesses the power to change your experiences by lowering the intensity and impact of negative emotions and turning up the volume of positive emotions and experiences, almost like the dial on a stereo.

Trigger Words

Some athletes use a type of code called trigger words. Trigger words are words or phrases that trigger certain reminders or emotions in the athlete. Athletes have used trigger words for decades.

Marathon runners count steps using the numbers as trigger words to maintain concentration.

Gymnasts might tell themselves to 'push' on the vault.

Basketball players or runners on the basepath in a baseball game might use trigger words like "be aggressive."

Golfers often select trigger phrases that result in desired body posture. For example, when taking a shot with a nine iron, a trigger phrase like "cut the grass" forces the player to keep his or her head down on the ball rather than a phrase like "follow-through" which would be more likely to draw the player's head up.

When Serena Williams defeated her sister Venus in 2002 at Wimbledon, she pulled out handwritten notes in between games. She told reporters after the match she had written notes for herself with the trigger words "stay low" and "hit in front."

To maximize efficacy, trigger words and phrases should be brief and worded in a positive way that encourages the pursuit, rather than the avoidance, of a particular behavior. Athletes should experiment during training with words that:

- Provide vivid imagery of success
- Instill confidence
- Drive concentration

Points to Remember

- To achieve flow during a competition, athletes must do everything in their power to put themselves on 'autopilot' by trusting their practice and training to take over.
- When a mistake is made in competition, it is critically important to let it go immediately.

- Athletes should examine their performance to identify the most common situations where they encounter difficulty and practice working through such situations during training exercises.
- Research suggests that an athlete's recall of information is facilitated by conditions that look, sound, and feel like those where the original training took place.
- Because athletics are heavily ritualized, successful athletes have realized that consistently engaging in preparatory rituals promote excellent performance. Consistent and repetitive training can't happen without motivation.
- Being able to focus is one thing. Focusing in the right way and on the right things is another.

3

VISUALIZATION AND MENTAL TRAINING

What Is Visualization?

Try this:

Go to a quiet place.

Focus your attention on your breath. As you inhale, follow your breath and imagine seeing it as it moves through your body, through your lungs, and back out through your exhalation.

Release any tension in your face and shoulders as you take each breath. With each breath, relax a little more.

Now, close your eyes as you continue breathing and focus on your breath until you are fully relaxed.

Open your eyes and continue this exercise.

Imagine yourself arriving at a competition, game, or match.

Where are you?

Who are you competing against?

What do you see?

What do you hear?

What do you feel?

What do you smell?

Now, see yourself performing at your very best. Perhaps at a level, you have not yet achieved. Be specific. See each skill being executed at the very best of your ability and maybe even beyond your current ability.

Close your eyes, continue to breathe slowly and deeply, and spend a good amount of time creating the experience from start to end. Once the experience is over, return to the breathing exercise and let the experience settle in your mind and throughout your body.

When you're ready, open your eyes.

Consider these questions. You might even want to write down your answers in a sports journal, which we will discuss later.

When you saw yourself performing, what did you see?

What was your physical posture like?

When you executed certain skills, how did that look?

What sounds were reassuring? What sounds were distracting or even threatening?

Examine the experience and review what you noticed.

This Is the Process of Visualization.

The process will be different for every athlete depending on the sport, the level of experience, the skills under construction, etc. However, the concept is generally the same across the board.

When athletes visualize, they purposefully and intentionally rehearse a skill, a routine, or a play in their mind's eye to feel the process of creating a successful outcome.

Whether you realize it or not, all athletes visualize in one way or another.

Our minds think using images. The way some athletes employ visualization can improve performance. In contrast, other athletes who unintentionally visualize improperly can cause damage to their performance.

An athlete who unknowingly replays their mistakes or missed opportunities repeatedly will only hurt their performance in the long run.

However, when athletes employ properly guided and intentional visualization, great results can be achieved.

Why Should We Visualize?

Mental imagery enables the athlete's mind to simulate a perfectly executed routine, throw to first, three-point shot, or shot on goal.

A gymnast will see herself executing the perfect gymnastics routine and feel herself nailing a steady landing. This process is used by many athletes to rehearse for competition cognitively.

It's more than just seeing the goal ahead of you. When athletes go into the future and live there in vivid detail for a bit, they can define their reality and essentially create a blueprint for what is possible.

When athletes visualize, they tap into the part of the brain that is later going to perform the actual physical activity.

Jordan Spieth

Some say that golfer Jordan Spieth won the Masters using visualization.

Spieth's coach since the age of 12, Cameron McCormick, has always been fascinated by how the brain works for elite athletes and considers himself a lifelong student of the mental game.

McCormick encouraged Spieth to visualize his shots and watch the shots of others and visualize those too. McCormick understood how activating what is known as mirror neurons would enable Spieth to mimic later the movement that would produce the desired results.

As athletes work to improve any skill - for Spieth, it is the golf swing - they create new neural pathways that trigger muscle memory. By activating these mirror neurons, athletes essentially learn in their minds before they learn with their bodies. Those mirror neurons can also be reactivated as you compete simply by watching your competitors or by visualizing yourself nailing that perfect shot.

Many coaches have followed McCormick's lead and now have their players write down their most memorable shots in golf or basketball, hits in baseball, or serves in tennis, and practice recalling them so the athlete can recreate these experiences in their minds and later with their bodies.

Spieth is known for visualizing and being incredibly fixated on his target. He can see a tiny branch on a tree to aim for. He'll then picture the trajectory of the ball and what shape it will take. He'll even see how the ball reacts when it lands.

Every one of these steps helps his body move in the right way to produce the desired outcome.

Research proves that practicing mental visualization improves skill learning and performance during competition.

Visualization stimulates the same regions of the brain that are activated during any physical exertion or completion—accordingly, visualization conditions the brain to automatically expect and operate at levels that produce successful outcomes. The more often an athlete's mind has rehearsed the optimal performance, the more ingrained the successful habits will become.

Professional athletes and their coaching staff give so much weight to visualization that it is not uncommon for teams to dedicate entire practice sessions to mental pregame walk-through.

What Are the Benefits?

All teams, from baseball to hockey, can employ visualization to rehearse or walk-through the desired skill execution the day before an important competition to reinforce skills and strategies.

Performance

Research proves that the mental activities athletes use to prepare themselves are just as important as the physical elements. Even your muscles benefit from visualization.

The brain can interpret visualization strategies in the same way it interprets the actual physical act. When athletes see themselves becoming stronger, faster, and more skilled, the mind helps the body make it happen.

Expectations

When athletes visualize themselves performing well in a competition and live that moment repeatedly, they tend to envision what might go wrong and what challenges to expect. By having the chance to think about ways to solve those problems in advance, the athlete can eliminate some unknown variables that can contribute to anxiety. The mind is then prepared to react to whatever comes its way. When you expect the unexpected, you have a better chance at controlling what might otherwise be an uncontrollable situation.

Confidence

Athletes can benefit from a boost in confidence through visualization. When you see yourself living your best performance, you are more likely to believe it is possible. Whether it's throwing that first-pitch strike, nailing that perfect landing, or defending the leading scorer like a beast, visualization allows you to see it and believe it.

Research proves that simply visualizing yourself receiving praise from a coach or teammates results in improved self-esteem.

Motivation

Visualization enables athletes to sustain motivation. Seeing your best self-accomplishing athletic performance provides an organic dose of inspiration. What you focus on becomes larger in your mind. Therefore, not only focusing on positive skill execution, positive results, and the desired outcome but seeing it and feeling it increases the likelihood of it happening. It's a natural producer of motivation that can get you through a particularly difficult workout or situation in competition.

Which Top Athletes Are Visualizing and What Have They Accomplished?

Athletes also use visualization and mental imagery to improve their ability to focus.

Michael Phelps

Let's talk about Michael Phelps. His habits have earned him the most Olympic gold medals of any athlete in history. One of those habits is mental imagery.

Phelps uses mental imagery to visualize and feel every stroke and turn within each race. His coach, Bob Bowman, required Phelps to run a mental video each morning and every night before turning in. Bowman wanted Phelps to see, feel, and hear every aspect of the race from how the starting block would feel on his feet to the sights and sounds of celebration after winning the race. Bowman would encourage Phelps to "play the tape" during training sessions.

Bowman said that this process enabled Phelps to "concentrate on these tiny moments of success and build them into mental triggers... It's more like his habits had taken over. The actual race was just another step in a pattern that started earlier that day and was nothing but victories. Winning became a natural extension" (Cohn, n.d.).

Lindsey Vonn

One of the greatest skiers in U.S, history, Olympic gold medalist Lindsey Vonn uses visualization in a very modern way.

Vonn, who began skiing at just three years old, loves using technology to advance her performance. She uses fitness trackers like the rest of us. Still, she wears wearable cameras to record performance from her point of view for later assessment purposes.

The technology that she finds the most useful is virtual reality. Its power is to take visualization to the next level.

Vonn feels visualization gives her a competitive edge because not every athlete taps into its limitless power.

"If everyone were given that opportunity to train -- to virtually train all the courses -- then it wouldn't be an advantage for me," she says with a laugh. "So I prefer if they wait a couple of years on that" (Guglielmo, 2015).

Vonn says that one thing she is good at is visualizing the course in her mind.

By the time she gets to the start gate, she has mentally run the race a hundred times, picturing exactly how she'll take each turn.

Once she visualizes the course, she never forgets it.

Vonn doesn't stop there, however. She is known to physically simulate the moves she plans to make by shifting her body in the way she plans to do it on the course. She even practices her breathing routine for competition as she is visualizing.

When there is no snow and no skiing, visualization allows Vonn to maintain all of this mental training still.

Arnold Schwarzenegger

Schwarzenegger is a bodybuilder who has always used visualization to reach his goals. For him, visualization is creating a vision of the athlete you want to become and then living and behaving as if you are already there.

"I had this fixed idea of growing a body like Reg Park's. The model was there in my mind; I only had to grow enough to fill it," he explained. "The more I focused in on this image and worked and grew, the more I saw it was real and possible for me to be like him" (Williams, n.d.).

Jack Nicklaus

Jack Nicklaus is a champion in a sport where visualization is big.

The golfer swears he has never swung the club, not even when practicing, without visualizing a focused image of what that swing will look like.

"First I see the ball where I want it to finish, nice and white and sitting up high on the bright green grass. Then the scene quickly changes, and I see the ball going there; its path, trajectory, and shape, even its behavior on landing" (Clarey, 2014).

Emily Cook

This aerial skier, two time Olympian, and five-time national champion shared how visualization impacted her team's experience at the 2014 Sochi Olympics.

At the starting gate, her entire team was visualizing as they prepared themselves to compete. "We're all up there, flapping our arms," Cook said. "It looks insane, but it works" (Clarey, 2014).

Although Winter Olympics are events where the environment is relatively controlled, Cook's sport of aerial skiing, where jump sequences can last up to 10 seconds, involves wind or weather patterns that can vary.

She and her team create imagery scripts and use scripted audio recordings to break down every element and every step to arrive at the exact jump she wanted to execute.

"I would say into the recorder: 'I'm standing on the top of the hill. I can feel the wind on the back of my neck. I can hear the crowd,'" Cook said. "Kind of going through all those different senses and then actually going through what I wanted to do for the perfect jump. I turn down the in-run. I stand up. I engage my core. I look at the top of the jump" (Clarey, 2014).

Cook plays the recording back for herself with eyes closed. She relaxes and feels each movement in her muscles. This mental work, she says, helped her become a better athlete.

Cook has used visualization for more than just competition.

She uses it to break negative thought patterns when she experiences them. The practice enables her to switch from negative to positive thoughts when at the starting gate.

She has also used visualization for healing purposes. When she suffered an injury that sidelined her for over two years, she and one of the U.S. team's nine sports psychologists at the Sochi Olympics, Nicole Detling, used visualization to see and feel her bones healing.

Billie Jean King

More than 40 years ago, Billie Jean King, winner of 20 Wimbledon titles, knew the power of visualization.

The tennis champion led the revolution for underpaid female players. It gained global notoriety during the 1973 exhibition match with Bobby Riggs, a notoriously self-proclaimed male chauvinist.

King used visualization to imagine anything that could go wrong and see herself reacting in an ideal manner. Whether it was the weather, a line call, or a delay, she tried to find examples of situations that would be out of her control and mentally see herself working through the problem.

"I would think about how I wanted to act. Like they teach in acting, 'act as if ...' — it's the same thing in sports. Do you stand up straight? Do you have your body language speaking confidently? Because 75% of the time when you're on the court, you're not hitting a ball. And I think that's where the champions come through. So I would visualize all these different possibilities" *(Pioneer Billie Jean King moved the baseline for women's tennis, 2014)*.

She would advise those she mentored to visualize themselves swinging the racket and hitting 50 forehand shots and 50 backhand shots in a row.

As she played, she focused on specific goals like returning serves to a particular spot on the court. In her visualization strategies, King always emphasized the importance of focusing on her performance on her side of the net. She visualized herself standing up straight, staying in the present moment, and immediately letting go of mistakes to remain present.

Mental Training

Earlier in this chapter, we touched upon the idea that everything we do is motivated by the desire to avoid pain or achieve pleasure. We also noted that the brain operates on associations rather than logic.

Let's now use this information and program the brain with associations.

Do you want to avoid a particular behavior? Teach the brain to associate it with pain.

If you'd like to stop staying up so late, associate late bedtime with pain—journal about the cost to you when you stay up late.

- Do you sleep later and miss a morning run?
- Do you find yourself feeling sluggish the next day and giving weaker effort during practice or workouts?
- Is your attitude more negative?
- What else are you missing out on by sleeping late?
- What other pain is being generated in your life?
- What does it cost?
- What else could you accomplish if you were up earlier and had more energy?
- How does it make you feel that you watched television instead of doing an activity that would make you feel productive?
- Calculate the number of hours of life you've missed out on by sleeping late.

Focus on all of the downsides of this behavior. Reread it later and add to it. The more you focus on the negative sides of the unwanted behavior and the more intense the feeling is, the sooner your brain will create an association between pain and staying up late.

The same is right about teaching the brain to associate pleasure with behaviors you want to nurture and experience more consistently.

Imagine you are a runner just starting. You always run two and a half miles. You know you can run three miles, but you never do. Journal about what running that extra half mile would be like.

- How accomplished would you feel?
- How motivated would you feel?
- How would your life be better if you increase your endurance?

- What athletic goals would become easier to achieve with this added endurance?
- Imagine yourself walking and cooling down at a different endpoint on your run with a confident smile.

Again, read the entry later and add to it. The more you focus on all the positive effects of this desired behavior, the sooner your brain will create an association between pleasure and running that extra distance.

Have fun with these exercises. Free yourself from your old beliefs and remember that your brain can be trained to remove limitations.

How Can Athletes Practice Mental Rehearsal?

When athletes arrive at the elite levels, every player there has the physical ability necessary to compete. What sets apart the athletes who will find real success is mental toughness.

Being able to master your thoughts and emotions after making a mistake and moving forward with confidence and composure is where the real power lies.

Mental training is a branch of sports psychology that focuses on helping athletes break through psychological barriers that prevent them from achieving peak performance.

Too many athletes and coaches resist or entirely disregard mental training because they don't understand it and therefore, can't see all of its benefits.

For athletes to optimize their performance and achieve their personal best, understanding mental training's value is critical.

Mental training will benefit the athlete by:

- Improving attitude and mental skills by identifying limiting beliefs
- Embracing healthy philosophies about their performance and their sport
- Addressing mental barriers like unrealistic expectations, fear of failure, and perfection

- Enhancing confidence and focus
- Building trust with coaches and trainers

Just like physical skills, mental skills require planning, commitment, repetition, and game-time application to be successful.

Begin With the End In Mind

You've likely heard that great planning begins with the end in mind. Almost like programming your GPS, you tell your brain this is where you want to go, and it will get you there. It's the same for athletics.

While planning for challenging situations is useful, and we will cite that as an important step, it's critical to begin the practice of visualization for athletic performance with the optimal outcome in mind.

See, feel, and hear your ideal athletic performance from start to end. During this step, train your mind to focus on only positive images. If you begin to play negative outcomes, be patient with yourself.

When practicing meditation, try to focus on your breathing and nothing else. If an unwanted thought enters your mind, calmly acknowledge it and send it on its way. Refocus yourself and begin again.

Call Upon Your Senses

See in vivid color. Whether you visualize the white strip down the basepath or the still water before your dive pierces it, see every aspect of your performance. Smell the victory. Smell the chalk in the gym, the smell of a newly opened can of tennis balls, or the chlorine of the pool as you visualize.

Hear the sounds, whether they are the positive cheering of the crowd or the negative calls from the opposing team's fans. Prepare yourself mentally to deal with anything that comes your way.

Feel the bat in your hands or the exhilaration of completing your longest or fastest run.

Internal and External Imagery

In the exercise at the beginning of the chapter, were you watching yourself as if in a video, essentially seeing your entire body as others would? Or were you seeing through your own eyes and from your perspective?

Maybe you alternated back and forth between these two perspectives.

Athletes can benefit from using internal imagery, sometimes called associated visualization, that leverages visualizing the experience through their own eyes and from their point of view. Athletes will find that this method enables a deep connection to the feelings involved during the visualization, critically important to the success of this strategy.

They should also explore external imagery, sometimes called disassociated visualization, where the athlete sees themselves from a third-person point of view or as if watching themselves on video. Benefits from this method can be found when athletes work through an event that was particularly difficult, deflating, or painful to gain perspective and wisdom. It can also help you achieving something outside of your current ability level.

Athletes can and should experiment to determine which method works best and the ideal combination of imagery methods for their particular needs. At different points in their athletic careers, the combination might change, so frequent reassessment is beneficial. Adapting the practice of visualization to align with new goals means you are using visualization effectively. It's an effective practice that all athletes should adopt.

Practice Visualization Consistently

If visualizing is not a regular practice in your athletic arsenal, you've probably tried meditating or visualizing only to find yourself daydreaming a few minutes in. That is a normal occurrence. Minds wander. Period.

Athletes who give up on visualization techniques are usually those that have not practiced enough or consistently enough.

The good news is every athlete can visualize effectively.

Visualization, just like meditation, is a mental muscle that becomes stronger when flexed and practiced. Treat this element of your mental training just as important as physical training. Schedule it into your everyday warm-up routine.

Visualize In a Relaxed State

Because athletes are typically under pressure when in competition, it's important to recall visualization techniques during stressful moments.

However, whenever possible, practicing visualization in a relaxed environment is most beneficial.

Call Upon Trigger Words

We discussed trigger words in our chapter about consistency and focus. Trigger words can also be very effective as an athlete employs visualization.

Some athletes imagine a red balloon filled with stress. The trigger word 'pop' helps them visualize a pin piercing the balloon and the stress slipping away. The athlete can remind themselves that using the trigger word or phrase can be used by the coach when necessary.

When trigger words are practiced in conjunction with visualization, it will be easy for the athlete to recall strategies that have been practiced.

Use Imagery Journals

Imagery journals can be used in a few ways.

Writing down the skills and execution specifics that an athlete desires can help maintain consistent visualization.

Logging how effectively the imagery is producing results is also helpful. For example, if a trigger word worked well in a game, recording the details will help solidify the concept in your mind.

Mental Toughness

Imagine a job where every time you make a mistake or something gets by you, a red siren blares, and the entire stadium stands up and screams. That's the life of a hockey goalie.

NHL goalie Matt O'Connor knows all about this. In his college days at Boston University (BU), his team made it to the Hockey East championship. A harmless shot by an opponent that he had routinely caught a million times slipped from his glove and fell between his legs. As he tried to retrieve it, he inadvertently knocked it into the goal. BU lost that game, and its hope for a championship was over.

So how did O'Connor recover from that devastating loss and go on to play in the NHL?

Mental toughness.

"Everybody gets scored upon," says Miller. "Maybe not quite as dramatically, or in the theater that this was, but everyone gets scored on. As a goalie, you have to learn how to let it go and get back to the present. The mantra is, 'Next shot. See it, and stop it.' That's all the goalie should be thinking" (O'Connor, 2015).

Mental toughness is about controlling the mind game. How athletes talk to themselves, maintain their composure, and eliminate distractions is critical.

Athletes must teach themselves a process that has no tolerance for a negative judgment. It's training yourself to move on to the next thing and seeing mistakes as part of the bigger picture that includes all of the times the athlete has executed positively.

After that championship game, O'Connor had to face reporters and answer questions about the mistake. This was an important first step in the test of his mental toughness. Understanding that being vulnerable and making mistakes is part of the athletic process strengthens the player as an athlete and as a human being.

Points to Remember

- When athletes visualize, they purposefully and intentionally rehearse a skill, a routine, or a play in their mind's eye in order and feel the process of creating a successful outcome.
- Research proves that the mental activities athletes use to prepare themselves are just as important as the physical elements. When athletes see themselves becoming stronger, faster, and more skilled, the mind helps the body make it happen.
- The brain operates on associations rather than logic.
- What sets apart the athletes who will find real success is mental toughness.

4

SLEEP, REST, AND RECOVER

If a trainer told an athlete about a new strategy that reduces hormones in the body associated with stress, naturally increases human growth hormone, speeds up recovery time, and is proven to improve performance, what do you think that athlete would say?

The athlete would likely say, "Where do I sign up?"

Sleep is that strategy.

Sleep, rest, and recovery are essential for athletic performance and overall well-being.

This information is not new.

However, its effectiveness is a new concept for many athletes.

What is also new is the attention that researchers and coaches are beginning to pay to the importance of sleep, rest, and recovery play in athletic performance.

In many sports, games are often decided by the little things - inches, one missed shot, etc.

Athletes go to great lengths to get that winning edge. Since they were young, their families spent thousands of dollars on equipment, trainers, and expensive elite travel teams. Professional athletes spend thousands of dollars on offseason training regimens. They exhibit superhuman self-control, sometimes cutting out sugar or power loading protein. NFL players have even been known to have installed hyperbaric oxygen chambers to promote faster recovery from injuries.

Isn't it surprising then, that the free and easy resource of sleep - that can be the difference-maker in these games of inches - isn't placed higher on the priority list?

This chapter will examine why coaches must understand the physical and psychological benefits that rest and recovery after training and competition provide. It will also examine how psychological recovery depends on high-quality sleep and periods of wakeful rest.

What Took so Long?

Although many professional athletes recognize the importance of rest for physical and mental well-being, coaches and trainers have been slow to guide optimal rest schedules and preventative and therapeutic strategies for achieving adequate sleep, rest, and recovery.

Research about best practices has produced very little useful information about rest. This is because the concept of rest, in general, has been overlooked when compared with sports psychology studies that focus on physical training and competition.

Explanations for this oversight include:

Rest is not exciting. The natural tendency is to focus on what is exciting. Let's face it. The inactivity associated with sleep, rest, and recovery is not as exciting as the physical actions required to execute the perfect play or to win the championship.

Stakeholders think they have no vested interest. The outcome of athletics (e.g., winning a competition or breaking a record) is important to all stakeholders. The seeming lack of correlation can cause it to be a low priority or not prioritized at all for stakeholders.

Out of sight, out of mind. Rest takes place behind the scenes, away from the training and competition site. It cannot be easy to value what cannot typically be observed and measured.

Rest is self-explanatory. To scientists and medical professionals who understand the intricate details of biology and cell repair, educating athletes about the benefits of rest and recovery might seem logical and worthwhile. Those who do not understand such things might consider rest to be too obvious, simple, and self-explanatory to include in an athlete's training program. When this happens, analysis of the concept falls off the radar.

Social lag has been largely ignored. A significant problem for collegiate and professional athletes has been swept under the rug for many years. Hangovers, or social lags as many call them, have a disruptive effect on sleep and, of course, on overall athletic performance. Believe it or not, alcohol use is widespread in the world of sports. Although many don't want to believe it or even acknowledge it, it is discussed a bit more openly as time goes on. However, research about the effects of alcohol on sleep and athletic performance is limited because of the sensitive nature of the topic and athletes' willingness to participate in such research.

Cultural norms generally undervalue rest. Society connects the dots between Type A personalities, overachievers, more work, and less sleep. The cultural and societal norms can subconsciously influence how people perceive the value of rest. Striving for goals, even unrealistic goals, tends to be highly valued in today's culture, and failure is thought to be something temporary, sometimes even self-imposed, that can be overcome by relentless hard work.

Athletic culture is often characterized by aggressive and competitive behavior, values results, and performance. Placing excessive importance on such dynamic values can cause athletes to feel lazy if they prioritize rest and recovery.

This last explanation has been particularly powerful in downplaying the benefits of rest and recovery. Research has found that athletes are often more motivated and disciplined when it comes to training than when putting forth effort toward healthy rest and sleep habits.

These researchers developed a strategy that labeled athletes who did not rest as lazy, since achieving adequate periods of rest and recovery time seemed to require more effort and self-discipline than the training itself.

Athletes will benefit from a better understanding of these reasons.

That better understanding can lead to an enhanced concentration of efforts toward learning about the benefits upon recovery, motor skill learning, and performance of rest.

Athletes have likely experienced some of the following as a result of insufficient rest:

- Physical and psychological fatigue
- Mood swings
- Performance decline
- Burnout

With an increased focus on and understanding of incorrect perceptions surrounding recovery, athletes can adjust habits and improve performance and overall well-being.

Why Is Sleep Important?

The correct quality and quantity of sleep protect mental health, physical health, quality of life, and safety.

When you sleep, your body works to keep your brain healthy and maintain physical well-being. It prepares the brain for the next day's activity. Sleep prepares the brain to form new pathways to support learning and remembering information.

For children and teens, sleep plays a significant role in physical, mental, and emotional growth.

Sleep is involved in the body's process of healing and repairing heart and blood vessels.

Sleep maintains hormonal balance. This is important for athletes because hormonal shifts can impact appetite, healthy nutrition, and energy.

Sleep also regulates how insulin impacts your body, your blood glucose levels, and energy.

The quality of sleep is important. Deep sleep triggers the release of a hormone that boosts muscle mass and helps cells and tissues repair themselves in children, teens, and adults.

An athlete's immune system relies on sleep to keep the body healthy.

Circadian Rhythm

Like breathing, the circadian rhythm is a pattern that is essential for the body. As in every other area of training, rhythm is important. The human body is designed to sync with rhythmic changes in the daily rhythms of light and dark changes.

In healthy athletes, physiological and biochemical variables such as body temperature, cortisol, melatonin, thyroid-stimulating hormone, noradrenaline, and serotonin show signs of the circadian rhythm. Disrupting circadian rhythm can decrease the production of natural testosterone and human growth hormone production.

Jet Lag and Social Lag

Daytime sleep can be a problem for athletes experiencing jet lag or social lag. Urges for daytime sleep results when you are tired. It's critically important for players to push through that urge and maintain active behavior. If enough hours are not spent active and out of bed during the day, the next night's sleep can also be interrupted. A negative pattern can easily emerge and interrupt well-established routines. Athletes should push through just as they would at practice and engage in physical activity outside in the natural light. Something as simple as walking can make the difference in getting sleep back on track.

Athletes must maintain a natural circadian rhythm. Jet lag and even the social lag from a late-night are part of life, and they are going to happen. If athletes properly plan for these types of interruptions, they can find their way back to circadian rhythm and regain the balance it provides.

In 2015, the New York Jets traveled to London to play the Miami Dolphins. The Jets were incredibly prepared. The fact that they packed their toilet paper was not the most interesting. They began preparing for the jet lag months in advance.

The Jets had to set the players' circadian rhythms five hours ahead, to Greenwich Mean Time. That's a tall order.

The general rule for overseas travel is that the body needs one day to adjust per time zone crossed. The Jets left New Jersey on a Thursday night. The game was going to be played Sunday afternoon in London. There were not enough days in between to adjust using the general rule.

Jim Maas, the retired Cornell professor who coined the term "power nap" a few decades ago and the sleep advisor for the Jets at the time, developed a plan.

The plan included rules that became increasingly important as the trip approached:

- "No caffeine after 2 p.m.
- No alcohol within three hours of bedtime.
- Keep room temperature between 65 and 68 degrees.
- Turn off or cover any blue, green or white lights in the bedroom, no matter how small.
- Nap for either 30 minutes, arising before you slip into deep sleep, or 90 minutes, after completing a sleep cycle, but never 60 minutes, because waking up in the middle of deep sleep can make you feel sluggish" (Mustard, 2015).

That was the simple stuff.

Each player arrived in his London hotel room and found a kit, purchased by the Jets for approximately $100, with orange-colored glasses. The glasses block the light from electronic devices that interfere with sleep. The players were instructed to wear orange glasses while using phones or studying film on tablets late at night. Players also used Litebooks, iPhone-sized devices that claim to reset circadian rhythms by waking the body up in the new time zone with a beam of 10,000-lux white light.

The Dolphins also put stock in sleep, but not to the same degree as the Jets. In Miami, the Dolphins' training facility in 2015 had a sleeping room with electronic relaxation systems.

The Jets won that game in London 27-14. Whether it was because of the orange glasses, no one will ever really know. It's safe to say it didn't hurt.

How Much Sleep Do Athletes Need?

The athletic performance of professional and amateur athletes alike can benefit from more sleep. The more you train, the more sleep you require. And due to the additional physical stress that athletic training places on your muscles and nervous system, your body needs more time to recover.

The exact amount of required sleep will vary from athlete to athlete, but eight to ten hours are generally recommended.

Roger Federer and LeBron James have reportedly been known to sleep on average 12 hours per night. Federer even once said, "If I don't sleep 11 to 12 hours per day, it's not right" (National Sleep Foundation, 2020).

What the Experts Say

According to the American Academy of Sleep Medicine:

- Adults require between seven and nine hours of sleep to optimize performance and health.
- Adolescents require additional sleep, ideally between eight and 10 hours.
- It has been suggested that athletes require nine to 10 hours of sleep to promote recovery between workouts.

The ideal amount of sleep will vary among different individuals depending on recent sleep history, age, exertion levels, illness, and stress factors.

Quantity vs. Quality

Quantity, or duration, is only one way to assess sleep. Sleep quality is also critical.

Recent guidance from the National Sleep Foundation indicates that sleep quality improves for athletes of all ages when sleep continuity is achieved. Sleep continuity is defined as routine bedtime and decreased nighttime awakenings.

How Does Sleep Deprivation Affect Performance?

The right quantity and quality of sleep at the right times can help athletes function at optimal levels.

However, athletes who are sleep deprived are less productive, have slower reaction times, make more mistakes, and put themselves in real danger.

Several nights of sleep loss — even as little as one to two hours per night — deteriorates a person's ability to function to the same degree as if they hadn't slept at all for a day or even two.

Lack of sleep can cause microsleep or brief moments of sleep that occur while awake.

If you have ever driven to practice and not remembered part of the drive, you may have experienced microsleep. Just as scary as driving while experiencing microsleep is practicing or playing a contact sport while experiencing microsleep. Athletes can miss critical information and put themselves in real danger.

Some athletes do not know at all about the risks associated with sleep deficiency. Many do not even know that they are sleep deficient.

Being sleep deficient can cause harm in an instant. An athlete can be distracted during a play or react slower than normal and sustain a devastating injury.

Sleep deficiency can also harm athletes over time. Making decisions, solving problems, and coping with change can become more difficult over time. Chronic health problems can also result from a persistent lack of sleep.

Children and teen athletes who are sleep deficient can experience problems getting along with others, which can impact the team dynamic. Tired athletes are more likely to experience more stress, feel angry, behave impulsively, and lack motivation. They also may have problems paying attention in class, get lower grades, and have trouble maintaining eligibility.

Sleep deficiency has also been linked to depression and risk-taking behavior, neither of which are positive factors for athletes.

A Proper Night's Sleep Does a Body Good

Researchers tracked the Stanford University basketball team for several months. The players added an average of two hours to their sleep totals each night. Here is what they learned:

- Players increased their speed by 5%
- Free throws were 9% more accurate
- Reflexes were firing faster
- Player felt happier

Other studies show similar benefits for football players and athletes involved in many other sports.

Another study of adult athletes included sleep journals before, and during, a national tournament to evaluate the relationship between sleep and competitive success. The two teams with the best performance and resulting highest placement in the tournament reported significantly more quality sleep duration.

Endurance Performance and Anaerobic Power

When compared to athletes who were sleep-deprived, well-rested athletes were able to achieve:

- Greater distance covered on a 30-minute self-paced treadmill test
- Increased time to exhaustion

- Improved rates of recovery between bouts of strenuous exercise
- More desirable pre-exercise muscle glycogen stores that may translate to improved endurance efforts

Accuracy and Reaction Time

When compared to athletes who were sleep-deprived, well-rested athletes were able to achieve:

- Better accuracy in tennis serving, basketball free throws, and three-point field goals
- Improved reaction times

Learning and Executive Function

The ability and capacity for learning are critical for athletic development, progress, and performance. Sleep is critical for learning, memory, and overall cognitive processing.

In the earliest cycles of sleep, blood flow to muscles increases, and the human growth hormone is naturally released. This enables the body to grow and cells to repair. New information or skills learned in practice that day, like strategies in film study, are organized and reviewed in their mind. As the athlete continues to sleep, the brain integrates those new skills and strategies with existing knowledge. The final 'lap' of sleep is characterized by bursts of brain activity that create new muscle memories from that day's activities.

It seems like a lot to miss out on by skimping on sleep.

These particular benefits of sleep extension are particularly crucial for children, teens, and collegiate athletes. They must satisfy athletic demands in conjunction with academic requirements.

When compared to sleep-deprived athletes, well-rested athletes were able to achieve:

- Improved neurocognitive performance, i.e., quicker decision making
- Completion of sports-specific tasks with greater ease
- Outcomes that required flexible thinking
- Better self-control and decision making
- Improved mood and decreased fatigue, soreness, depression, and confusion

Sleep Tips

Athletes tend to overestimate the amount of sleep they get. One way to ensure an adequate amount of sleep is to plan. Strategize just as you would for a workout. Setting routines and establishing boundaries as outlined in the following tips will go a long way in ensuring that athletes get the amount of sleep they need.

Off Days

Dealing with sleep on your off days isn't as easy as it sounds. A day spent in bed doesn't necessarily add up to a well-rested athlete.

Winding down from a practice or a game is not easy. Athletes know they need rest, but not all rest and recovery strategies are equal. Managing downtime is just as important as managing schedules for training and competition if an athlete wants to optimize performance.

Collegiate and professional athletes might be tempted to celebrate and enjoy their celebrity status on days off. However, when it's time to get back to work, designing a plan for enjoying yourself, although it might sound crazy, is the way to go. How an athlete deals with their downtime is what separates the good from the great when it's time to train and compete again.

Acknowledging social lag, preparing for it, and knowing how to recover can mitigate performance disruptions without being a major buzzkill.

What the Pros Do

If you are skeptical about putting forth the effort to rest properly, think about these NFL teams and the lengths to which they have gone to prioritize sleep for their players.

- The Miami Dolphins and the New England Patriots have added dark rooms to their practice facilities to take naps.
- The Philadelphia Eagles players complete a morning questionnaire on their tablets, self-reporting how long they slept the previous night.
- When linebacker Demario Davis arrives at the Jets headquarters at 6 a.m. to study film, he studies in the glow of a team-issued Litebook. This space-age device maintains circadian rhythm by promoting alertness with a beam of white light with the same intensity as natural sunlight.

Everyday Tips

Athletes can take action to improve sleep habits. To improve sleep habits, athletes should:

- Go to bed and wake up at the same time every day. Maintain a consistent sleep schedule on weeknights and weekends.
- Integrate early morning and afternoon exercise to help maintain or even reset a healthy sleep-wake cycle by raising body temperature early enough in the day and allowing it to drop and trigger sleepiness later gradually.
- Use the hour before bed for quiet time. To the extent possible, adjust training schedules to avoid strenuous exercise at night.
- Avoid large meals before bedtime.
- Remember that the effects of caffeine can last as long as eight hours. A cup of tea or coffee at 2 p.m. can be a bad idea.
- Keep your bedroom quiet, cool, and dark. Eyeshades or blackout curtains can help.

- Consider a relaxation routine like meditation or a shower before bed to signal to your brain that it's time to wind down.
- Journal or list-write any concerns about upcoming training or competition events to help clear your mind before turning in.
- Keep a separate sleep diary to record behavior and sleep success outcomes. This can help identify patterns on nights where your sleep was ideal so you can replicate those patterns, and nights where you had difficulty so you can avoid those patterns.
- Limit naps. Take them earlier in the afternoon and for no more than 20 minutes.

Some athletes who struggle with achieving the proper rest are choosing to monitor their sleep patterns and carefully make changes in their diet, routines, and other habits. Athletes know that what can be measured can be managed. There are many strategies and even sleep tracking devices that can help. Athletes with persistent complaints of poor sleep or excessive daytime fatigue should consider additional measures, including:

- Screening for preexisting medical conditions such as insomnia, sleep-disordered breathing, restless legs syndrome, depression, anxiety, or concomitant illness.
- Adjusting training, sleep, and wake times before traveling to other time zones to incrementally 'practice' sleeping in the time zone of the destination. This is done to potentially shorten the required amount of sleep adjustment time upon arrival.

Athletes who prioritize regularly scheduled and well-structured rest time, even on their days off, can maintain and also improve performance without damaging their social lives. Consistent monitoring and measuring is the only way to manage sleep, rest, and recovery, and it is the key to gaining that competitive edge over competitors who don't prioritize these important elements of their craft.

Points to Remember

- Coaches must understand the physical and psychological benefits that rest and recovery after training and competition provide.
- With an increased focus on and understanding of incorrect perceptions surrounding recovery, athletes can adjust habits and improve performance and overall well-being.
- Athletes know that what can be measured can be managed.

5

HEALTHY EATING TO FUEL YOUR BODY

Physics and nutrition are not often discussed together, but perhaps they should be?

Newton's laws of motion tell athletes that objects remain at rest, or in the same patterns unless they are compelled to change their state by external actions or elements.

The external element, in this case, is nutrition. When athletes see nutrition as a force that can change their state, they may begin to place more weight on its importance.

However, nutrition books can be complicated and time-consuming. Often they are too scientific to be practical or helpful. Professional athletes rely on science and have teams of experts doing all of that dirty work for them. They also rely on common-sense practices that work.

The value of food for athletes should never be judged by how much attention it is getting in pop culture. Nutrition should be the logical application of what athletes know about themselves and the primary scientific benefits of food.

See what different athletes are doing to enable nutrition—this external element—to impact the pattern within their actions and emotions.

Athletes understand that the physiology of athletic performance is not just based on energy production. An athlete's success requires proper nutrition for growth and continued development of muscles, mental function, and the immune system to fuel that energy production.

Professional athletes work with nutrition experts whose knowledge of the power behind the relations between carbs, fat, and protein has exponentially increased in the past few years and continues to do so every day. These experts advise athletes and develop personalized plans to consume balanced diets, hydrate properly, and tap into micronutrients from various foods to maximize performance.

This chapter will explore what professional athletes are learning from their nutritional advisors and will allow you to choose which plan makes the most sense.

Why Is It Important to Fuel Your Body?

The body burns energy during daily activity and exercise. Food and liquids replenish the body's energy. Energy balance happens when you exert the same amount of energy as you consume. Sounds simple, right?

For athletes and especially those still in adolescence, a variety of other factors must be considered.

Increased nutritional needs

As an athlete's body mass grows, it requires more calories to maintain that energy. More intense workouts burn more calories, but athletes don't always compensate by increasing their caloric intake to account for the additional activity.

Nutritional information is lacking or misinformed

Athletes and parents often lack specific nutritional knowledge. It can be difficult without expert guidance to separate valid information from incorrect information.

Overscheduling interferes with meal planning

After practice, it's all too easy for athletes to grab a quick burger or skip dinner altogether. Planning amidst a busy schedule is critical if athletes consume an adequate number of calories from nutritional sources.

Fad or sustainability-conscious diets

Athletes who choose to become vegan, vegetarian, or gluten-free, among other dietary programs, might not appropriately plan for making up for lost calories and nutrients that are essential for the increased activity level in an athletic lifestyle such as calcium, protein, iron, or vitamin B-12.

Body image

Athletes are not immune to distorted thoughts about body image. The impacts upon diet and calorie restriction must be carefully considered and monitored to avoid serious nutritional deficiencies. Clinical eating disorders like bulimia and anorexia are certainly severe issues. The most prevalent problem common among athletes is consuming too few calories or calories that are not nutrient-dense enough to support rigorous athletic routines and performance.

Digestion

Whether you're an amateur runner, working out to lose some weight, or you are in the middle of a grueling season, intense workouts can impact your digestive system and put stress on your immune system. It's essential to pay attention to how you fuel your body and find the right combination of carbohydrates, protein, fat, vitamins, minerals, and fluids to maintain healthy digestion.

Tom Brady

The TB12 Diet

The NFL legend has a new diet named after him called the TB12 Diet that is sometimes called the Tom Brady Diet.

The diet is largely composed of whole foods, and Brady attributes it to his football longevity. The diet has been said to lower the risk of injury, improve athletic performance, and drive recovery rates and energy levels.

The diet, which is not based on scientific facts, has been criticized for its unnecessary complexity. Critics also claim it is unsustainable in the long term.

Brady wrote a book in 2017 called the TB12 method that details 12 principles he uses for sustained athletic performance and excellence.

Like other diets, TB12 emphasizes eating whole foods that have been minimally processed and recommends avoiding foods that are believed to be acidifying or inflammatory. The diet promotes a variety of TB12 meals, snacks, and proprietary supplements.

This method combines the principles of other diets like the alkaline diet and the Mediterranean diet by promoting organic, locally grown, seasonal, and minimally processed foods.

The Rules

The majority of recommended foods for this diet, 80% to be exact, should come from organically grown fruits, vegetables, whole grains, nuts, seeds, and legumes. The remaining portion of the diet comes from lean meats that should meet several criteria. Fish must be wild-caught, and meat must be not only organic, antibiotic-free, and hormone-free but also from grass-fed animals.

Those on this diet are encouraged to avoid anything that might be acidifying or cause inflammation. Among those restricted items are dairy, most oils, foods containing soy and gluten, as well as nightshade vegetables like potatoes, peppers, and eggplant. As you may have guessed, food containing sugars, artificial sweeteners, trans fats, caffeine, MSG, and iodized salt are also off-limits, as is alcohol.

As if all of these guidelines weren't enough, Brady's plan also restricts combining foods. For example, fruits should not be eaten with other foods. High-protein foods like meat or fish should not be eaten with food rich in carbohydrates like sweet potatoes. Water should be avoided during, before, and after meals. However, it is necessary to drink a significant amount during the day.

Sample Menu

If you're left wondering what an athlete would eat this way, here is a sample meal plan:

Breakfast: Homemade granola stirred into coconut yogurt.

Lunch: Hearty vegetable-chicken soup with kale and brown rice vermicelli.

Dinner: Wild salmon tacos on GMO-free corn tortilla wraps served with a side green salad.

Aly Raisman

Aly Raisman last competed in the Olympics in 2016. The gold medal gymnast has since become a vocal advocate for sexual assault survivors and a supporter of the body positivity movement.

Raisman knows what routines can do to the lifestyle of an athlete. Although her diet was much more structured in 2016, she still considers herself an athlete and maintains an athlete's diet. The athlete in her thinks about food in terms of what will keep her most energized for the activity ahead.

Keeping It Simple

These days, Raisman's diet is largely plant-based. She says she eats what makes her feel good. It's as simple as that.

Her day begins with a glass of celery juice. Then she'll typically have hot water with lemon. If she opts for coffee, she'll add soy milk as she finds even the slightest bit of protein makes a difference for her considering the plant-based diet.

The Menu

After meditation or another form of exercise, she'll take a break for a mid-morning snack, which might be a seedy bagel or a bagel with nuts, again keeping an eye on the protein. Another snacking option for Raisman is cauliflower rice with sliced avocado.

For lunch, Aly often opts for vegetable broths and soups like broccoli and spirulina soup. By making a big batch, she can save herself time and have it for days.

Afternoon snacks might be her homemade guacamole or a smoothie. Smoothies can be different every day. Her latest ingredient is ashwagandha powder. Aly usually combines mixed berries, hemp hearts, a little soy milk, and chia seeds to create a powerful, protein-packed beverage. The supplement has been said to provide multiple benefits, including lowering cortisol, soothing joint pain, boosting memory, lowering blood sugar, and building muscle. It's important to note that the supplement is not for everyone, however. Some studies report that it can cause miscarriage.

Dinner is usually a heavy plate of veggies, although Raisman might include fish. Her go-to dinner is a plate of oven-roasted potatoes with a side of greens, like cucumbers and brussel sprouts.

She doesn't deprive herself of dessert, although she does keep it healthy and plant-based. She treated herself with frozen bananas blended with soy milk and topped with dairy-free chocolate chips.

Rashad Jennings

This former NFL running back who played for the New York Giants, the Oakland Raiders, and the Jacksonville Jaguars has a busy schedule and is often traveling, but he always prioritizes clean eating.

Jennings' diet is both gluten-free and dairy-free.

Gluten-Free Lifestyle

Gluten-free diets are becoming increasingly popular with athletes. As the research is mostly inconclusive, gluten-free popularity needs to be carefully reviewed, along with the effects of gluten-free diets on athletic performance.

A survey of 910 Australian athletes reported that 41% are following gluten-free diets or trying to reduce gluten intake by more than 50%. The diet is so popular because many athletes experience gastrointestinal issues and believe the symptoms are caused by gluten.

Half of the athletes who used a gluten-free diet in the study reported an improvement in gastrointestinal symptoms that were sometimes combined with additional symptoms like fatigue. However, a double-blind study (participants did not know which diet they were on) of 13 endurance cyclists revealed no differences in gastrointestinal symptoms or overall well-being.

Some nutritionists urge athletes, especially those with increased caloric requirements during endurance training, to consider that they might be exposing themselves to nutrient deficiencies by choosing a gluten-free diet.

The Science Experiment

The gluten-free lifestyle works for this 35-year-old athlete, who recently competed in Dancing with the Stars. Jennings places a great deal of importance on being aware of what you put into your body since it will directly impact the results you are trying to achieve.

You might be wondering how a professional athlete like Jennings does not eat bread.

In high school, Jennings says he was an overweight kid with asthma who was a fifth-string running back. A high school coach eventually talked to him about his weight.

The self-described 'dork' tried an experiment. He left a McDonald's hamburger, some cheese, milk, and bread on the counter for three days. Next to that, he placed a plate of chicken, lettuce, and an unpeeled banana. After three days, the hamburger, cheese, milk, and bread had become thick and hard, while the chicken, lettuce, and banana had only slightly - and naturally - deteriorated. He put two and two together and figured if that's what's happening outside his body, the same was likely to be happening within.

This informal science project caused Jennings to begin a quest for more information. He met with doctors and nutritionists to learn more about healthy eating and ultimately decided to stop eating gluten.

The rest is history: Jennings went on to play Division 1 football in college before being drafted by the Jacksonville Jaguars in 2009. Now, he is an advocate for healthy eating, the Meatless Monday campaign, and works to spread the importance of nutrition through the Rashad Jennings Foundation.

The Menu

To achieve his personal best, Jennings plans out each meal with a personal chef and takes prepackaged meals on the road when his busy lifestyle has him traveling.

Jennings also incorporates a good deal of exercise into his routine, so his caloric intake exceeds 4,000 calories. Here is a sample meal plan he recently shared with Sports Illustrated:

Breakfast

Protein Shake: 2 scoops of Garden of Life vegan protein powder, ¼ cup organic rolled oats, 1 tbsp. organic raw flax seeds, one organic banana, 1 tbsp. organic peanut butter, 1 tbsp. organic coconut oil & 1 cup organic unsweetened almond milk.

Lunch

Turmeric chicken: 8 oz. organic free-range chicken (with skin on), 1 cup sautéed vegetables (carrots, sweet peppers, green beans), ½ cup jasmine turmeric rice.

Herb grilled chicken baby green salad with organic cilantro lime avocado dressing: 3 oz. organic free-range boneless skinless chicken, 1.5 oz. organic baby greens, 3 oz. assorted raw veggies, 3 oz. organic cilantro lime avocado dressing.

Blueberries and almonds: 6 oz. organic raw blueberries, 3 oz. organic raw almonds.

Dinner

Coconut crusted salmon: 8 oz. wild-caught coho salmon, 1 cup steamed organic broccoli, 5 oz. roasted sweet potato.

Herb grilled chicken baby green salad with organic cilantro lime avocado dressing: 3 oz. organic free-range boneless skinless chicken, 1.5 oz. organic baby greens, 3 oz. assorted raw veggies, 3 oz. organic cilantro lime avocado dressing.

Apple and almonds: 1 organic gala apple, 3 oz. organic raw almonds.

Snacks

Organic coconut crusted chicken fingers: 4 oz. organic free-range boneless skinless chicken fingers and 2 oz. organic BBQ sauce.

Kristin Armstrong

World-renowned professional cyclist Kristin Armstrong focuses on balance to properly fuel her body while actively training.

Carefully Planned Meals and Snacks

When preparing to fuel an athlete's body while in training mode, it is key to design and adhere to a plan. Many athletes unintentionally make poor choices when it comes to nutrition because they didn't plan.

With trophies, medals, and championships on the line, that seems silly.

Armstrong never skips breakfast and eats three daily balanced meals as well as a few nutritious snacks and doesn't eliminate any food groups. She maintains variety by mixing different carbohydrates, proteins, fruits, and vegetables into every meal and snack. She's lucky to have no food allergies, which allows her more freedom when designing her nutrition plan.

Keeping things simple is important. Armstrong is a mom and leads by example, so her family also thinks about fueling the body like an engine and seeing healthy foods as enablers for the body to make it operate stronger and faster.

Taking time to plan meals helps athletes manage cravings and avoid potential dietary pitfalls that result from impulsive decisions made by a hungry brain regarding food and drinks.

Breakfast Every Day

For many years, studies have focused on the importance of breakfast for good nutrition. Athletes especially require calories in the morning to fuel recovery and exercise. Breakfast boosts blood sugar, endurance, and performance.

Armstrong stresses the importance of breakfast in setting athletes up for success and shares that knowledge with her family.

Lots of Liquids

Athletes know they must remain hydrated, but proper hydration can be elusive when training is especially hard.

Even the slightest bit of dehydration can impact performance. Severe dehydration can be life-threatening.

For casual hydration throughout the day, Armstrong again keeps it simple with regular tap water and carbonated water with natural flavoring.

When drinking with meals or while on the bike things, she takes a different approach.

"I drink milk with my meals and make sure that when I am out training on my bike, my bottles are filled with a mix of water and electrolytes," she added. "Many sports drinks are very high in sugar and calories — it is important to know when to use [certain drinks], as well as which ones are beneficial to your performance" (Macey, n.d.).

Athletes can find sources of hydration in foods like the following healthy options:

- Oatmeal
- Fruits and vegetables
- Low-fat vanilla yogurt
- Low-fat milk

Fueling up Before Workouts

Athletes who skip meals can harm their bodies.

"If you begin skipping meals it sets your body back, and it will not be able to manage the workload and demands you place on it throughout the day," said Armstrong.

Regular meals and snacks are part of Armstrong's day. She eats snacks for both training and pleasure. She doesn't think denying temptation all the time is a good thing for athletes.

"On-the-bike snacking or fueling is also important. After 60 to 90 minutes of aerobic exercise your glycogen levels become depleted; it is important to refuel these energy stores if your training session is longer than this," Armstrong said.

She continued, "If I have a sweet tooth, my go-to is fruit; I make it the easy choice by stocking my refrigerator with a variety of choices. If I don't grab some fruit, some of my other favorites are yogurt, cheese, or a glass of chocolate milk."

Eat to Recover

Athletes looking to prepare their bodies from the inside out must plan for proper recovery.

Sleep and its importance for athletic recovery are covered in the previous chapter. However, decisions athletes make during the day about their diets can help the body recover more effectively at night.

Armstrong incorporates a focus on recovery into every workout.

She shared, "There is a 30-minute window post-training where I focus on my recovery. This is done through a protein drink or natural foods such as plain yogurt with honey or maple syrup. The larger meal can come within a few hours post workout."

Points to Remember

- An athlete's success requires proper nutrition for growth and continued development of muscles, mental function, and the immune system.
- The value of food for athletes should never be judged by how much attention it gets. Nutrition should be the logical application of what athletes know about themselves combined with the basic scientific benefits of food.

6

IMPROVE YOUR AWARENESS

Journaling

Richard Kent instructs a group of high school students to create an entry in their journals. Some of them like it and furiously fill line after line. Some of them struggle, looking off into space lost in thought or boredom.

It might sound like an English class, but they sit on the soccer field after a big game.

Kent, a former English teacher, uses this opportunity to allow students to process and unpack the game that was just played. He guides them with a series of prompts to analyze the strengths and weaknesses, the team, and the opponent.

They are instructed to visualize adjustments that should be made for future games.

The players, even those who don't enjoy writing, seem to take it seriously because they understand that journaling is real work that can make a difference in their game.

Kent uses journaling to organize his athletes' training goals and organize their reflections about their performance. His teams have even been known to write when journals are not available. One team used airsickness bags on a flight back from England.

Athletes in every sport and of every performance level can benefit from journaling to learn about themselves and their sport. Kent finds a correlation between each of the following activities and the benefits of writing about them:

- Watching and debriefing practice and game film
- Studying the team playbook
- Reading articles, blogs, websites, and books
- Making mistakes
- Listening to interviews with professional athletes
- Visualizing
- Competing
- Preparation, control, and routine
- Self-encouragement
- Balance and alignment
- Downtime and playfulness (Kent, 2014)

Benefits of Journaling

Organization

Journals enable athletes to organize, plan, and reflect.

It's easy for an athlete to forget why exactly they are training. Journaling about goals and new strategies can help athletes organize their intentions to focus on the bigger picture.

Athletes can then use journals as evidence for further self-reflection. When an athlete records a daily workout and dietary intake for that day and then records a journal entry at the end of the day, the athlete can begin making connections between activity and outcome.

When journals are used as a tool of reference, athletes can begin to see their achievements and reflect upon how their hard work has paid dividends. They can also identify strategies that work during games or competition and those that did not.

Motivation

Journaling helps athletes learn about patterns of motivation, energy, and fatigue. They find out what they know and, more importantly, what they don't know.

Knowing that a journal entry will follow a workout or a game can help athletes stay the course and sustain motivation and commitment. The added accountability increases the likelihood that athletes will push themselves during training.

Journaling also increases the ability to self-regulate behavior to accomplish carefully planned goals. By putting off immediate gratification in favor of long-term accomplishments and benefits, athletes can see how this discipline pays off as time goes on.

Confidence

When it's time to compete, journals provide athletes the opportunity to reflect on how dedicated they were to their training commitments and have faith that they did everything to prepare themselves.

Positive thinking and confidence go hand in hand. Journals can be used to develop positive affirmations and develop strategies for deploying positive thinking.

Emotional balance

As athletes write, they connect further with their experiences and future experiences on the horizon. They are not only looking backward, but they are solving problems and learning about themselves. As athletes face negative emotions, they reduce anxiety and develop strategies to manage those emotions by increasing self-awareness. This naturally leads to development.

Journals lend perspective. Too often, athletes can obsess over a poor performance or training session. Journals help vent that frustration, put it behind them, and identify patterns before, during, and after a poor performance.

Venting frustration is an important element in maintaining emotional balance. Athletes might not want to share the challenges and even the achievements associated with their sport with family, friends, or even teammates. A journal can provide the perfect outlet for working through these emotions.

Physical balance

Journals can help athletes break through physical plateaus by evaluating performance and enhancing their future approach to achieve new levels of success.

Preventative and reflective efforts are also important in maintaining physical balance for athletes.

Journals can help prevent overtraining. When athletes become more aware of their physical state after a workout or competition through writing, they can recognize when it might be time to lighten up on training.

Journals can also provide insight into patterns that may have contributed to an injury.

Different Ways to Journal

There are many ways to journal. One size does not fit all. Athletes should feel free to use a variety of methods or stick with just one that works.

Simple bulleted lists. Include time and place of training and details like distance, reps, or sets. Rate your effort, energy levels, meals, sleep quality the night before, and motivation.

Preparation. Athletes can benefit from journals to prepare themselves for competition. Questions like the following can put you in the right frame of mind to achieve your personal best:

- What am I looking forward to?
- What am I grateful for?
- When something goes wrong, how am I going to react?
- How will I keep myself in the moment?
- What mantra or cue words am I going to call upon?

Reflection. Describe how the training felt. Include details about feelings afterward - both emotional and physical. Describe your thought process and recovery process, as well as any muscle soreness. Comment on the effects of nutritional variations on performance.

Prompts. A coach or trainer can provide prompts. Athletes can also find many prompts through a quick internet search, or they can develop their own.

- On days I'm not feeling my best, did I make a few bad eating decisions?
- Am I overestimating or underestimating my training?
- On days where I felt particularly focused and effective, what routine did I follow?
- How did my use of cue words work today? Where could I have used them but forgot?

Routine entries. Some athletes prefer a consistent approach that requires no creativity. They simply address the same items in each entry. For example, they might answer these three questions in each entry:

1. What worked well today?
2. What went wrong?
3. Anything else worth noting?

Free write. For some athletes, just writing in a stream-of-consciousness format is most effective. The entire entry does not have to be focused on the training or the competition. Elements from your personal life might very well be impacting your performance, so examining those issues and working through them can certainly be helpful.

Drawings or diagrams. Athletes who don't enjoy writing can supplement or replace words entirely with drawings or diagrams to reflect or prepare themselves for competition. This can be particularly effective for younger athletes.

Professional Athletes Who Journal

Curt Schilling. The Boston Red Sox pitcher has been known to record pitches to many batters and the effectiveness of those pitches in between innings. He includes details of the scenarios at work. Of course, he could reflect later by watching back the game, but recording his feelings at the moment likely provides additional insights that may have been lost if he had waited until after the game to reflect.

Serena Williams. During her victory at Wimbledon 2007, Williams shared a few pages of her journal. Some of the entries were as simple as only one sentence:

- "My good thoughts are powerful.
- My only negative thoughts are weak.
- Decide what you want to be, have, do and think thoughts of it.
- Hang on to the thought of what you want. Make it absolutely clear.
- You will look at balls.
- You will move up.
- You're #1.
- You are the best.
- You will add spin.
- Turn FAST.
- You will have long follow throughs.
- You will win Wimbledon" (Writing Athletes, n.d.).

Listen to Your Body

Receiving advice like "listen to your body" can feel nebulous. What does it mean?

It means having self-awareness, physically, mentally, and emotionally. Self-awareness means cultivating the ability to make yourself the subject of your awareness. Study after study over the past 50 years shows that attention can be focused outward on the environment or inward on yourself, but awareness cannot be focused on both at the same time.

To listen to your body, you need to develop the ability to become present and identify extremely subtle changes within yourself. This requires becoming aligned with yourself and attentive to your breathing, your heartbeat, your digestion, your mental state, and your physical state.

Successful athletes leave very little to chance for skill development, nutrition, or fitness, so why would you leave the more subtle aspects of the physical or mental game to chance? The more you know yourself, the more you can control yourself. The more variables you can control, the better control you're likely to have over your performance outcome.

It also means knowing your strengths and weaknesses inside and out and developing strategies that accentuate those strengths to compensate for those weaknesses. Tennis great Steffi Graf was doing this every time she ran around a backhand shot to maximize her forehand. You won't see Shaquille O'Neal going for many three-pointers instead of staying near the net to use his size and force to dunk on the opposition nearly every time.

When athletes learn how to do these things, they can learn what to expect before, during, and after training and competing. This can provide a sense of calm and control.

Make no mistake. This process is not a quick and easy one. Becoming introspective is difficult and takes time to master. When coaches ask questions like "What is holding you back?" many athletes have a hard time answering. Being honest about your weak spots is hard and requires real honesty and trust.

Listening to your body is particularly important when recovering from an injury. Too often, athletes want to speed up their recovery to avoid letting their teammates down. However, by going back to the game before the body is fully recovered, athletes can put themselves and their athletic careers at even higher risk. Listening to your body can help prevent this. Listen and trust what your body is telling you.

How Does It Work?

Identify your blind spots. Start by asking others - coaches, teammates, parents - for honest feedback. Ask them what you might be missing, both physically and mentally. Ask how you could be a better teammate. Ask what aspect of the game they think you can put more effort into. Watch videos and do some real self-assessment and reflection to understand their feedback.

Listen to your inner voice. We all run a script in our heads. What kind of self-talk do you hear? Is it positive and encouraging, or is it negative and chronically critical? When you learn something new or develop a new skill, what kind of script do you use to motivate yourself?

If you find that your inner voice is intensely negative, action needs to be taken to reframe that voice. First, you must identify when you tend to use negative self-talk. Is it under pressure? Is it after a mistake? Once you identify the patterns, replace negative self-talk with language that reflects a growth mindset. For example, instead of saying, "I suck at this," try tapping into a growth mindset that will sound more like "With practice and determination, I will improve." Try channeling the pressure that caused the negative self-talk in the first place into other pre-practice routines or other rituals.

Are you present? How effective are you at letting things go? When you make a mistake, are you holding on to it an hour later, or do you know how to let it go and stay present?

If you need work here, consider meditation. Focus is a mental muscle that requires practice and discipline just like any other muscle in the body. Find some quiet time and try just one minute of clearing your mind and breathing in and out. Try to think of nothing else except breathing in and out. When a random thought comes fluttering by - and it will - gently acknowledge it and guide your mind back to your breath. Eventually, with more practice, the amount of time between those fluttering thoughts will get longer and longer. As those periods extend, so will your ability to keep the mind in the present moment rather than focusing on a mistake you made in that last game.

Journals are a great tool to support this process.

Awareness

Many athletes expect the repetition of physical practice to develop the correct habits and ensure the right outcome.

If it were this easy, everyone would be a professional athlete.

The mind resists developing new habits. It doesn't like to do it. It often produces the wrong responses, and players who don't focus on awareness and training the mind will continue to miss the mark during competition and suffer by putting effort only towards physical practice.

For practice to be effective and result in improvement, athletes must focus on awareness. To become more aware, athletes need to identify their patterns of:

- Entertaining negative thoughts.
- Allowing the mind to be hijacked and controlled by the wrong emotions.
- Stifling the flow of positive energy or cutting it off altogether by continuing without a mental training strategy.

By operating using bad habits, athletes ingrain these habits into their physical performance and become their own worst enemies.

Have you ever had one of these negative thoughts:

- I can't beat this player, or we can't beat this team.
- We always lose when we play in this field.
- We always lose in overtime.

- When I fault on the first serve, I'm always less confident on the second one.
- I never have energy at evening practice.

Of course, you have had these thoughts. Every athlete has. Even though athletes might be ashamed to admit that these thoughts are ever entertained, it's human to have ideas like these and many others that enter your mind. We all know negative thinking can do irreparable damage to all of the time, energy, and effort put towards our athletic training. Athletes know negative thoughts can lead to negative performance. Unfortunately, negative thoughts are a part of life. It happens.

Here is the more important question: Are you aware of the thought when it occurs, how it persists, and how it impacts your attitude and performance?

Probably not so much.

When you become aware of these thoughts, you can keep them at bay. What's more, you can cultivate habits that encourage positive thoughts to replace them. When athletes develop awareness around their thinking, they open up endless possibilities.

The journals that were discussed earlier are the perfect place to develop awareness.

Ask yourself at the beginning of each day, questions like:

- What challenges am I expecting today?
- How will I treat them when they present themselves?
- What positive attributes do I possess to solve problems that arise?
- In what other times in my life have I overcome obstacles?

Do it every day. Yes, every day. Even answering one of these questions will begin to develop the mental muscle for awareness. If you answer one question and only spend two minutes on it, your brain will begin to expect this kind of question at the beginning of the day. The more you make it routine, the more likely you will be to call upon these practical solutions when encountering negative thoughts.

When those negative thoughts enter your mind - and they will - be easy on yourself. Acknowledge the thought, congratulate yourself for recognizing it - even if it took an hour of letting it bounce around in your subconscious - and send it on its way.

Becoming aware of the negative thoughts is a huge first step to ridding yourself of their power over you as an athlete.

Once you can identify them, you can then begin replacing them with powerful positive thoughts like we discussed in Chapter 3.

Again, use that journal to prepare yourself with some positive thought replacements like:

- I need to think like a warrior to win.
- What positive things can I focus on right now?
- It's the better player who wins; it's the player who plays better.

That last thought leads to the next point about awareness.

Fixed Mindset vs. Growth Mindset

Becoming aware of how the brain operates and directing your thinking is another powerful strategy for athletes looking for more control over their performance.

Those with a growth mindset believe that ability can be developed. Athletes with a growth mindset understand that they can improve through hard work and create healthy habits and effective strategies.

Athletes with a fixed mindset believe that their athletic ability is a fixed trait that is mostly unchangeable.

An athlete's beliefs about their athletic ability have significant consequences for how they experience training and competition, and how they respond to setbacks and adversity. Athletes with a fixed mindset can avoid challenges, give up more easily when faced with a struggle, and end their athletic careers because of false beliefs about their ability and potential.

Athletes with a growth mindset see challenges as opportunities to grow and are more likely to embrace those challenges to push themselves beyond current perceived limitations and thereby train harder and compete better.

Here are some examples.

Example 1

Put aside the fixed mindset, which says:

My teammates are using their time to get in extra weight lifting training, but I am too exhausted to do anything but go home and eat dinner.

Shift your focus to a growth mindset, and try:

It's okay that I'm not at that extra weight lifting session. What I need right now are food and rest. I'll get a good night's sleep, and I'll be able to join the extra session tomorrow.

Example 2

Instead of using the fixed mindset, which says:

I never make the starting lineup. My coach must think I'm just not good enough.

Shift your focus to a growth mindset, and try:

My coach just doesn't know what I'm capable of yet. I'm going to journal tonight and develop three new goals to achieve that will demonstrate my commitment to my coach and help him see me in a new light.

Example 3

Instead of using the fixed mindset, which says:

My batting average will never be as good as my teammate's batting average.

Shift your focus to a growth mindset, and try:

I can learn new strategies and new techniques to improve my batting average. I have made progress in being decisive and patient at the plate, and I can make the same progress with my swing. When I do make it on base, I add so much to the team as a base runner.

Being aware of these two mindsets will enable athletes to realize there is a choice. Becoming aware of choosing a growth mindset each day brings athletes closer to mastering control over more of their potential.

Resilience

Awareness is particularly important when an athlete encounters a setback. Whether it is an injury, a goal left unachieved, or athletes must address a major loss, resilience, and the awareness of its importance.

Resilience isn't something we're born with. Some athletes were never taught about it, and even if they were, it isn't something that happens overnight. Resilience is a set of coping mechanisms that athletes develop over time. Performance is largely determined not by our circumstances or an athlete's genetic makeup but by an athlete's actions.

Some athletes just aren't aware of how much control they do have in how resilient they are or can be.

Again, resilience and awareness of it can be developed through journal writing. Writing about a setback, rather than just replaying it in your mind, can help make sense. By realizing that the setback hasn't caused the world to end and recognize your ability to maintain your daily routines, you develop your resilience.

Journaling about the path forward, the necessary steps to take, and where that path can lead is an integral part in the development of resilience. Journal entries don't need to be perfect. It's okay if you haven't figured out exactly what the next steps are. The important part is opening your mind to the possibilities instead of dwelling on the setback.

Sometimes the setback is so significant that progress may be difficult. Again, that's okay. Even if you do only one item each day to move forward, that is something. Being flexible is part of being resilient.

Gratitude also plays a part in resilience. Using your journal to list items for which you're grateful helps to play up those items and diminish the setback's effect by reducing feelings of hopelessness and powerlessness. Resilience is about maintaining hope and restoring power.

When working towards becoming more resilient in the face of a setback, don't be afraid to ask for help. Becoming a resilient athlete doesn't mean you have to handle everything alone. Talk to teammates or coaches to help reshape your perspective about the setback and the path forward.

The Importance of Breathing

Breathing. It's involuntary. It's something we do every day often without thinking. As a result, it often doesn't get the amount of attention it deserves when it comes to athletic performance. However, the benefits that proper breathing can provide are staggering and should not be overlooked.

When athletes concentrate on slower, more effective breathing on and off the field, they can experience tremendous results.

Reduced anxiety. The body is always striving to achieve homeostasis or equilibrium. Because athletic performance is continuously working against that equilibrium by pushing the body in and out of cardiorespiratory challenges, athletes can help achieve that equilibrium when at rest or off the field entirely through breathing. Athletes who practice meditation and deep breathing exercises can ward off anxiety, depression, insomnia, and digestive issues.

Improved focus. When breathing slows down intentionally, heart rhythms stabilize and allow the mind to focus. Consider pairing deep breathing exercises when practicing the visualization techniques previously discussed in the book.

Increased endurance. Athletes who practice breathing through a variety of very simple techniques will feel the difference at the end of the workout and in the last minutes of competition. Instead of losing steam and momentum, athletes will be able to push harder through the end.

Better blood flow. While stretching at the end of a workout, athletes who breathe properly increase the amount of blood pumped back into the heart. When this happens, the body experiences many benefits, including disposing of toxins and metabolic waste produced during the exertion of energy.

How Can I Do It?

There are several easy ways to incorporate proper breathing techniques into your training and competition playbook.

Six BPM. This is six breaths per minute. Pretty simple, right? This breathing rate promotes heart rate to increase inhalation and decrease respiration, resulting in a lower overall heart rate. The ultimate goal here is for athletes to be able to access this strategy during competition on demand. When they feel pressure, they simply pull up the go-to strategy to center their minds and move toward optimal performance.

Six BPM is the goal. Smaller steps will help athletes get there. In all of the smaller steps breathing through the nose is the key to achieving the benefits of proper breathing.

Athletes who need a broken down strategy into smaller pieces can benefit from these simple exercises to build up to it over time.

Ten count. This simple technique helps beginners focus energy on their breath and get started with focusing on the practice of intentional breathing. Just like when you meditate, try to only focus on the breath.

Breathe in. Breathe out. One.

Breathe in. Breathe out. Two.

All the way to ten.

Try it.

If you got distracted, like many of us do at first, that's normal. Forgive yourself and try again.

Bend and breathe. Bend forward from your waist as far as you can in a comfortable way and place the palms of your hands on your lower back. As you inhale and exhale, see how many seconds you can count on each inhale and on each exhale.

Again, if you get distracted, just start over.

Head to toe. This is a breathing technique you can practice as you fall asleep. Lay on your back with your eyes closed. Slow your breathing. Focus your attention on your head. Dedicate one cycle of breath to focus on relaxing your forehead. Next, move to your eyes. Dedicate another cycle of breath here, noticing the tension in your eyes and intentionally let them relax. Continue this process with each cycle of breath. You might fall asleep, which is completely fine.

The ultimate goal here is to begin to train yourself to notice the breath and its power, so that come game time, you can call upon it to support you.

Points to Remember

- When athletes develop awareness around their thinking, they open up endless possibilities.
- When journals are used as a tool of reference, athletes can begin to see their achievements and reflect upon how their hard work has paid dividends.
- They can also identify strategies that work and those that do not.
- The more you know yourself, the more you can control yourself. The more variables you can control, the better control you're likely to have over your performance outcome.
- Athletes who become aware of negative thoughts can keep them at bay and cultivate positive thoughts to replace them.
- An athlete's beliefs about their athletic ability have significant consequences when it comes to how they experience training and competition and how they respond to setbacks and adversity.

7

BUILD YOUR NETWORK

Once the Los Angeles Lakers coach, Pat Riley, is infamous for conducting practice that is five times harder than the exertion during an actual game. Riley understood that games are won or lost in that last quarter, and the team with the endurance is likely to prevail.

In the old days, a coach could tell a team to run through a wall and do it. Today, athletes who are often treated like royalty need a different kind of motivation.

Even with the intense practice, Riley asked for 25% more from the players. The players pushed back, and Riley's team was about to go off the rails. Riley went to motivational coach Tony Robbins for help.

Robbins advised Riley to go back to the team and apologize. Gulp. Riley did not jump at this suggestion at first. He did not like the idea, but he followed the advice of Robbins.

Riley apologized and told the team that they really couldn't get much better. Following Robbins' advice, he asked for just 1% more. The players looked at each other and scoffed at the 1%, knowing they were capable of much more, as if to say *we can do way better than that, watch us.*

Having a coach or a trainer who is willing to seek advice from others, swallow their pride, apologize, and try new strategies is essential. Building a network of people on whom you can rely can be the difference between a career that thrives and fizzles.

Surround Yourself With the Right Training Partners

In the past few decades, group training has become an international trend as spin cycling, aerobic, and dance-based exercise classes have all become wildly popular. The emergence and rapid success of concepts like CrossFit indicate how effective exercising with a pack mentality can enhance athletic performance.

Research shows that healthy exercise habits, decisions, and actions of others can be a very good influence. Athletes gravitate towards the exercise behaviors of those around them. Surrounding yourself with those who make good decisions and those who are a few steps ahead of you is a good idea.

Surrounding yourself with the right people is important in all walks of life, especially in your athletic development. Exercising with someone else is good. Exercising with someone more advanced than you is even better.

Here are five questions to ask yourself when considering who is the best training partner for you.

1. Is this person's ability level similar to mine?
2. Can I learn from this person's strengths?
3. Do this person and I have similar goals?
4. Does this person have the right attitude?
5. Does this person train the way I want to train (this question is not about whether the person trains the way I train now, but how I want to train in my ideal world)?

The Benefits

Drive commitment. Of course, you will look for training partners that give as much as you do, and maybe even more. You'll have more energy to face athletic challenges when support goes both ways.

When you work out with the right people, you will experience benefits that drive motivation, consistency, and duration. When you work out with others, it's likely part of an implied contract. You have committed to showing up with your best effort for one another. Positive peer pressure from others will increase your commitment to training.

Athletes are typically committed to their development, but sometimes it can be not easy to achieve consistency and maximize commitment to training schedules and routines. When athletes have training partners depending on them, accountability kicks in, and commitment levels rise.

Intensify effort. You would likely agree that nobody wants to be the weakest link in a group setting. This idea has a name. It is called the Kohler effect. For athletes and those exploring fitness, the Kohler effect means you are more likely to push yourself harder when working out with people who are more advanced or fit.

A study proved that those who worked out with a more capable partner improved their best plank time by 24%. The motivational gain of the more competent partner pushed the participants in the study beyond limits that otherwise would have held them back.

In every group, there is always that person who becomes the 'reach' or the 'goal' for the group.

You are likely to work out longer and harder if you are working out with the right people. Studies by the Society of Behavioral Medicine confirm that working out with a partner improved performance and time spent exercising. Results were even better for those who worked out with a group in a team format. Some doubled their workout time compared to those who exercised alone.

Highly effective athletes opt for group workouts a few times per week to push themselves toward their personal best efforts and outcomes.

Grab that competitive edge. Let's be honest. When your teammate, friend, or even a stranger is running beside you, the inherently competitive nature inside every athlete causes you to push yourself harder. This kind of competitiveness is positive.

You can become inspired to work harder, do more, and even find new ways to exercise. You might also learn something about yourself that you hadn't previously realized. You may have avoided trying a new routine or strategy, but working out with others helps you learn to be more flexible and willing to pivot. This can open the door for substantial growth opportunities.

Exponentially boost endorphins. Workouts with others are more fun. Someone is likely to yell some encouraging words. A little encouragement goes a long way during a workout. A few shouts from partners to do one more rep or one more quarter mile can be just what you need. When one of the weaker group members is having an especially good day, the positive vibes begin flowing and become infectious. The mental advantages of a group workout are great for morale. You've heard of the runner's high and already know that working out, even when alone, boosts endorphins. When you add the social element of a group workout, now you are releasing endorphins in different ways.

You are more likely to smile around others, and that boosts endorphins.

Someone tells a joke during a workout, and that boosts endorphins.

The above mentioned additional commitment and intensified effort that results from working out with others make you feel better and more accomplished. That also boosts endorphins.

Provide new perspectives. Seeing training, progress, and competition from different points of view can support resilience and awareness. Surrounding yourself with partners and teammates with a positive attitude helps you focus on the possibility of growth. Partners also see you differently than you see yourself and can help you gain the confidence to break outdated or unwanted habits and patterns. They can also help you visualize possibilities.

Relieve stress. Social support has been studied and proven to be a powerful predictor of happiness, health, longevity, success, and resilience. Surrounding yourself with the right people as you train and compete can act as a buffer to reduce stress and promote your ability to cope with challenges.

The personal connections we make with others are suitable for the soul. When athletes train with teammates or workout partners, they report feeling calmer and enjoying the workout more than when training alone. Time flies when you are having fun, so the group workout is likely to last longer and provide you with added stress relief and endurance.

Diversify your routine. Variety is said to be the spice of life. The same holds for athletic training. Training partners bring fresh new ideas to a workout, but working out in pairs or groups extends the spectrum of exercises possible. You can now make more moves like medicine ball toss sit-ups and relay cardio routines.

You now have someone to heighten the safety of your workout by spotting you. Still, you can lift a heavier load, and you also have someone to troubleshoot your form and help you realign to achieve your best results.

Avoid training partners that are reluctant to expand their horizons. You need partners who will help you look for new ways to develop as an athlete. Since it's exactly those new strategies, exercises, and approaches that forge new brain connections that enable you to push through plateaus and adapt when faced with a setback, these are the types of partners you are seeking.

Add accountability. Athletes who train with others often report being able to accomplish things they never thought were possible until a training partner or teammate pushed them through a physical or emotional plateau. Athletes create a bond with one another because pushing yourself involves a certain degree of vulnerability. Exposing this part of oneself develops camaraderie that leads to accountability that is always good for overall athletic achievement.

Family and Friends

One of the most famous athletes of all time, Tiger Woods, was trained from a young age by his father. Earl Woods used many different strategies with Tiger, one of which was cursing quite explicitly during Tiger's backswing. It might be an unorthodox approach, but Tiger swears it helped him enormously throughout his golf career and even through personal trials and tribulations. Earl Woods knew Tiger would have to maintain an unparalleled focus to become competitive and successful. Tiger often claims to see but not see and to hear but not hear because of those exercises.

Michael Jordan's family also had a significant impact on his work ethic and his athletic perseverance. His father, a maintenance worker, built Jordan a basketball court in the backyard of their home. His mother, a bank teller, was the rule enforcer and instilled the drive to succeed in her son. Larry Jordan, Michael's older brother, gets credit for the all-star's competitive side. The two played out back on that court until bedtime every day.

Jordan Spieth finds support from his family in a different way. He can appreciate the game no matter how he plays. Spieth attributes this attitude of gratitude, which helps take the pressure off, to having a sister with special needs. Her ability to be happy despite the struggles she faces helps him maintain perspective and realize how lucky he is to tee it up for a living.

These are the success stories.

We know that not every player will be the next Tiger Woods, Michael Jordan, or Jordan Spieth. Unfortunately, many parents have yet to realize this fact.

Parent Involvement in Youth Sports

It is all too often that signs at youth athletic fields have to remind parents of the proper ways to behave at their children's sporting events. Signs display instructions like:

1. These are kids.
2. This is a game.
3. The coaches are volunteers.
4. The umpire is human.

5. Your kid does not play for the Yankees.

In the past few decades, sports have become an opportunity for parents to live vicariously through their children. Sports are also seen as an investment to many parents, many of whom believe this investment may lead to a college scholarship. Parents start their kids in sports earlier and earlier. Some even begin as toddlers, next playing on expensive travel teams, and spending a large portion of childhood traveling to and from private coaching, practice, and competitive tournaments.

Life in many aspects is all about keeping up with the Joneses, and youth sports are no different for many parents.

There are many different arguments for and against this new approach to youth sports. The most significant question parents should ask is: What does my child want?

A recent study at George Washington University surveyed nearly 150 children about what they found fun about sports and why so many are quitting. Kids identified 81 factors contributing to their happiness. You can probably guess that tournament play and expensive equipment was low on the list. Positive team dynamics, learning, and positive coaching topped the list.

Parents and coaches often don't want to hear about these types of findings.

Parent Involvement in Olympic Sports

Olympic athletes can turn to people outside of their team and training circle for support. Friends and family members can provide emotional and mental backup, but they can also cause emotional and mental strain.

The 2008 U.S. Olympic diving team knows this first hand. One of the coaches, Chris Carr, is now a sports and performance psychologist. Carr and his colleagues held workshops for divers' family and friends before the Olympics to teach them how to optimize support and minimize distraction.

As elite athletes train to become Olympians, their parents often require just as much training to transform themselves into Olympians' parents. Sports psychologists don't only support the athletes anymore. Sports psychologists also counsel the athletes' families to develop a family dynamic that nurtures the athlete's performance and achievement and maintains their emotional balance.

Parents can struggle to figure out what the best type and amount of involvement looks like. Parents know how to provide financial support and logistical support for their athletes, but the emotional support piece is the tricky. Parents often fall into one of two situations:

- When athletes struggle with physically, psychologically, and emotionally demanding schedules, pressure, and responsibilities, parents can find themselves unequipped or unprepared to help.
- Other parents might over provide, and their support might extend to an unhealthy approach or amount that piles on top of the stress the athlete is already under. Parents who blur the line between where they end and where the athlete's life begins can become a distraction for their children.

Sports psychologists can help parents maintain their composure and provide athletes with tools to help parents if that is the most effective. Parents should be optimistic and supportive of their children. Leave the performance, the score, and the standings to the coach.

Seek Professional Help

Sports Psychologists

Athletes have a different mindset than they once did.

Have you ever seen a character in an action film who gets an electrical shock and is blasted across the room?

It's easy to think that the shock is what propelled that person across the room. In reality, the electrical impulse causes all the fibers in the body's muscles to twitch at once. The body throws itself across the room.

That tells you something about the amount of power contained in the human body.

How does this relate to sports psychologists?

The brain acts as a limiter to that power and essentially prevents us from accessing all of that power. It might be a natural protectant, so we don't hurt ourselves by tearing muscles and ligaments.

The more we learn about the brain and how it limits the human body, the more we become able to peel back those limits.

Sports psychologists help athletes to convince the brain to peel back its limits.

Endurance activity was once thought to be harmful to the body. Still, now we know that the body is designed for endurance. This knowledge inspires athletes toward bigger and more challenging feats.

Sports psychologists change the mindset of athletes and open the door for athletes to understand what they are truly capable of.

Sports Physiologists

Sports physiologists study how physical activity affects the body. Coaches and trainers are sometimes physiologists, but some athletes work with physiology specialists. These professionals can help athletes optimize performance, recover from injury, prevent injury, and learn proper technique.

The role of physiology can contribute to the optimal preparation for athletes. Athletes undergo a series of tests in a climate-controlled environment chamber. The physiologists can adjust the climate to reflect what the athlete is likely to encounter during competition. For example, athletes competing in the Summer Olympics in the southern hemisphere will test in temperatures within the range for the predicted time of year.

Based on test results, physiologists can advise athletes how to train optimally and advise coaches to adjust training schedules accordingly.

Physiologists will collate specific test results for each athlete that ultimately contribute to the design of optimal workouts for that particular athlete.

For example, the tests might include:

- Checking how much sweat is lost in certain climate conditions.
- Attaching sweat patches to see which chemicals in which amounts are present in the sweat to adjust hydration strategies to maintain fluid balance and electrolyte levels.
- Assessing which energy sources are utilized during exercise.
- Testing gas exchange to measure thresholds for physical preparedness and peak performance.
- Analyzing pulmonary oxygen uptake to determine how much oxygen is being used and how much carbon dioxide is being produced in various scenarios to understand the burn ratio of carbohydrates to fat.
- Employing near-infrared devices that analyze how proteins deliver oxygen to the body to identify what exercise intensity does to various muscle groups.

All of this data is then used to prescribe the most effective training routine.

Points to Remember

- Surrounding yourself with the right people is important in all walks of life, but especially so in your athletic development.
- Having a coach, trainer, or training partner who is willing to seek advice from others, swallow their pride, apologize, and try new strategies is essential.

- Parents know how to provide financial support and logistical support for their athletes—take care with emotional support.
- Sports psychologists can help parents maintain their composure and can also provide athletes with tools to help their parents if required.
- The more we learn about the brain and how it powers and limits the human body, the more we can fuel that power and peel back those limits.

8

BELIEVE IN YOURSELF

Andre Agassi was one of the first athletes that worked with Tony Robbins. He had been number one in the world and won Wimbledon. He then experienced a fall from grace when he injured his wrist and then encountered a series of losses. He was considering quitting the sport.

Tony Robbins worked with Agassi. Agassi was skeptical. Robbins asked if Agassi had ever hit a tennis ball perfectly. He asked him to visualize himself, hitting the ball perfectly ten times. Robbins watched as Agassi, with eyes closed, began to smile as he envisioned this. Agassi said he was not thinking about his wrist at all as he visualized.

They both watched a video of Agassi winning at Wimbledon. They watched Agassi walk onto the court with complete confidence. Robbins called his body language prowling. Agassi admitted that he was thinking to himself about his opponent, "Why did you even show up?"

Robbins and Agassi then watched a video of Agassi after a series of losses. The body language had changed. Robbins pointed out that Agassi was not the same man.

Robbins was trying to prove that the athlete with greater certainty and confidence will always achieve greater success.

How Do You Achieve Certainty?

Physiology and focus play a role that is greater than most people realize.

Energy makes that difference. To shift energy, athletes must create momentum. Once you create or change momentum, your game will change.

You take action, and you believe it will happen. Close the gap between potential and results by understanding that certainty is everything.

Too often, you can see an athlete walk out onto the field and know whether they have certainty or don't.

Consider this example. A kicker walks out onto the field to kick a field goal. He has little certainty. The body language reflects it. The ability to execute is deflated.

This chapter will examine how that kicker can change the results in advance by using his mind to change his state.

What Is Self-Confidence?

If you sometimes feel that everyone but you is sure of themselves and confident, you are not alone. It's very likely that these people doubt themselves and have insecurities.

So why do they seem so confident?

The answer is likely straightforward. They realize that confidence is not about knowing it all or a trait that you have, but it is something that you work hard to create. Being confident is the certainty that you can accomplish anything you set your mind and energy to.

There is a certain level of trust you must have in yourself to believe - believe - that you can navigate your way to a successful outcome regardless of the situation.

What Are the Benefits of Being Self-Confident?

Perseverance. During those times, when athletes feel like giving up, confidence can be the lifeline that pulls them through. Confidence gets you through the toughest training, the games where your team is trailing, the times where you are simply outmatched by an opponent, or when a teammate takes your spot on the roster.

Perception. Coaches and teammates don't look to athletes who are consistently unsure of themselves. To be a productive part of any team, you need to present confidence during even the most difficult of situations.

Relationship building. By fostering maturity and overcoming insecurity, confidence will help athletes handle relationship conflicts with teammates, trainers, and coaches, and solve problems that arise.

How to Improve Self-Confidence

To become more confident, you must change your state.

Athletes, like all other human beings, have emotional patterns. Your state is your mental or emotional pattern at any given point in time. These mental or emotional conditions tend to influence the way we see life.

The great news is that you can change your state anytime, anywhere, no matter what.

Learning to change your state is one of the greatest - and simplest - gifts an athlete can give themselves.

You need to know how to do it.

The Story

The first step is the story we all tell ourselves. We all have that story. We tell ourselves what we are really like, what we are capable of, and where our limits begin. We tell ourselves we can do these things, but not those. The dangerous or powerful part about this is that we are usually right. It all comes down to the story that we tell ourselves. The great news is that you are in charge of that story.

Tell yourself a story where the things you hope for and dream about are possible, and you're usually going to be right.

Tell yourself a story where those things are out of your reach, or you don't deserve them, and guess what? You're usually going to be right.

You know those people who say, "I'm just not a runner." They never became runners, did they?

Don't let your story limit you. Let your story lift your state and your certainty about what you can achieve.

Here is the question: If you have the freedom to write your own story, what will you write?

The Strategies

Body language. Think of someone you consider to be unwaveringly confident. How would you describe them? When they enter a room, how do they behave? How do they carry themselves? How do they walk? What kind of eye contact do they make? What type of posture do they have?

For those seeking confidence, the phrase "fake it until you make it" can get the ball rolling. In other words, act like you're confident. Right now, try it. Stand up straighter, pull your shoulders back, and control your breathing. Mastering your body language is critical to becoming more confident.

Your physiology can radically change your mood, your state, and your confidence.

Positive thinking. Where your focus goes, your energy tends to follow. What you focus on becomes bigger. These are all sayings that you have probably heard before. Do you know why you've heard them? You've heard them because they are true.

The mind can only focus on a small piece of experience. The good news is that you can condition your brain to seek the positive pieces of your experience.

Consider when you buy a new pair of running sneakers, and all of a sudden, you begin to notice those sneakers everywhere. Did everyone buy them when you did? Of course not. Your brain has been conditioned to look for them by spending a small amount of time concentrating on them during purchase.

The mind's reticular activating system (RAS) programs your brain to pay attention to certain things. Mental conditioning helps lead the RAS in paying attention to the positive visualization elements you are seeking. The RAS acts as a customs checkpoint and determines what is going to get through to your mind and what is going to be turned away.

Try it. Think about an upcoming practice. Let's say you had your best sprint time ever, but also had a problem with a coach at the last practice. The piece of that memory on which you choose to focus will become bigger in your mind. Give it a try.

Focus on the sprint time. You see yourself running. You feel your blood pumping, hear your heart beating, feel the wind on your face, and the exhilaration of beating your personal best time. You're probably feeling pretty good right about now.

Now focus on the problem with your coach. Relive the argument, your side of the story, and how you may have been understood. Feeling some anxiety building up? You're probably not feeling so great.

When you practice daily conditioning to decide what you want, you can begin to use your mind and positive thinking as a conditioning tool, just like you would a muscle-building supplement.

How can you do this?

Use affirmations paired with physical movement and feeling to create a level of certainty in your entire body. Decide what you want and condition yourself daily. Find role models. Write down the specific skills that you are seeking to develop or improve. Then seek out role models - either those you know or professional athletes that you can read about - and do what they do. Decide to commit on a large scale and in an intelligent way.

What you focus on becomes bigger. Again, the great news is that you are in control of that choice.

Positive thinking can manifest itself in different ways. Instead of obsessing about how things might go wrong, focus your attention and visual imagery on all the good things.

Replace negative images, predictions, and self-talk with more positive thoughts and seek out the best possibilities when your mind begins working.

When you change your focus, you are changing the future by changing your state.

Growth mindset. A fixed mindset thinks that your skillset is, as the name indicates, fixed, and nothing can be done to change it. A growth mindset thinks that your skillset is dynamic and can be changed over time.

The fixed mindset thinks, "I suck at this." The growth mindset thinks, "With practice, I can improve and do better in the future."

Many people think that confidence develops from prior experiences - prior success in particular. The misconception that you can only be confident after you've achieved success is incorrect and severely limiting. Sure, confidence can be strengthened through success, but it initially comes from within.

Operating with a growth mindset means knowing that when you fail, you can and will brush yourself off and try again as many times as it takes.

Gratitude. When was the last time you stopped to be thankful for your body and your health that make it possible to be an athlete? How about being thankful that you live in a place in the world where it is safe enough to participate in recreational activities like athletics?

Practicing gratitude can help develop confidence in several ways.

First, how you feel about yourself affects the way you behave. When you appreciate all that is positive about yourself, you naturally build healthy self-esteem and confidence.

Second, gratitude boosts confidence by decreasing the potential for envious feelings or jealousy. Instead of wanting the winning record of a rival team or the starting spot on your team, you focus more on yourself and what is within your control and begin to recognize and focus on the progress only you can influence.

This is a perfect opportunity to use your journal. A gratitude journal is an ideal place to record three items each day for which you are grateful. For example:

1. A coach that goes out of her way to play motivational music for us.
2. The smell of the freshly cut grass at practice today.
3. Feeling my muscles relax as we stretched after practice and being grateful I have no injuries or pain.

Visualize success. Even the most seemingly confident people experience times of insecurity and doubt. When you notice these feelings begin to creep in, visualize a recent accomplishment or a future event having a wildly successful outcome. See yourself being as confident as possible and know that executing in that manner is well within your reach.

Power pose. We all have inner power. Athletes can increase confidence by tapping into that inner power. During times of uncertainty, remind yourself of this power by having a power pose at the ready.

Develop the pose that helps you reconnect with your inner power. Yoga poses like Warrior One or Warrior Two are especially effective. If you're not a yogi, try either of these easy poses:

- Standing with your hands on your hips and your feet shoulder-width apart.
- Standing with your head held high, your back straight, and your arms stretch high overhead.

The pose itself is not as important as the deep breaths you take and the positive images you visualize as you strike the pose to connect with your inner strength.

Breathing. Stress is a drain on an athlete's confidence. Stress and toxins can be alleviated by taking a full deep breath. Take an intentional deep breath that fills your lungs and slowly release the breath. By doing this simple act, athletes can radically decrease the stress and anxiety that can be draining on energy and confidence.

Exercises to Increase Confidence

Exercise 1: High-Low Table

Understanding what causes your confidence to fluctuate is important in achieving greater confidence stability.

- Divide a piece of paper into two columns, labeling the first column, "high-confidence situations," and the second "low-confidence situations."
- In the first column, list situations in your sport where you feel entirely confident.
- In the second column, list the situations in which you lack confidence.

Exercise 2: The Spotlight

Visualizing your state during successful experiences in which you have felt high degrees of confidence can help maintain those feelings and help you tap into them during times of insecurity.

- Imagine a spotlight shining down a few feet in front of you.
- See yourself in the spotlight performing in one of the situations from the first column in the previous exercise.
- Visualize yourself performing at your peak level of athletic performance. As we discussed earlier, explore each of your senses.

Exercise 3: Positive Affirmations

Positive affirmations, or self-talk, will deepen your confidence.

Knowing that you believe in yourself and your skills and abilities is a simple step that many athletes overlook.

- Develop statements that you truly believe about yourself. Examples include: "Nobody's getting by me" (defensive linesman); "Just me and the catcher's mitt" (baseball pitcher); "Be aggressive" (baserunner)
- Practice whichever affirmations you choose before bed and when you wake in the morning. Repeat them as you train and in the shower. Use them as a distraction from negative thoughts or in times of anxious feelings.
- Most importantly, use them during games or competitions.

Exercise 4: Spin the Mix

Music can calm the savage beast. It can also inspire, motivate, and boost confidence. Athletes from all sports utilize music to help improve their confidence and performance.

Whether you are motivated by the lyrics, the beat, or other associations, music is a healthy athletic tool.

Athletes choose music to instill confidence in different ways. Consider variables like:

- Is there music that reminds you of an optimal past result?
- What is speaking to you at this particular moment?
- Which songs pump you up? Which songs calm you down?
- What works for teammates? What works for top athletes?

The key to choosing the right music for you is understanding how you need the music to motivate you. Then test your choices while warming up or during practice. See what makes you feel confident and ready to tackle whatever comes your way.

Anchoring

You have likely heard about Pavlov and his dog. Pavlov conditioned dogs to drool whenever he would ring a bell. This was possible because the dogs became conditioned to associate the bell with food.

Pavlov was using a technique of Neuro-Linguistic Programming, or NLP. NLP is learning to speak the language that appeals to your particular mind. In essence, Pavlov was speaking the dog's language and creating deep associations between cause and effect.

NLP considers the conscious mind to be responsible for goal setting and the subconscious mind responsible for goal getting.

Within NLP is a strategy called anchoring, which enables you to create associations that have a motivational effect on your mind.

You probably have a song that makes you feel psyched and motivated to practice. That song is the anchor to accessing that motivation in your mind. Anchoring provides you with the chance to place an emotional order, just like at a restaurant. You want something, you order it, and it comes. By creating your anchors, you can create desired emotional outcomes.

Imagine being able to create a feeling of total calm and a feeling of centeredness by merely pushing your thumb and pointer finger together. Replace calm with whatever emotion you'd like and replace the physical stimulus of pushing fingers together with any other stimulus you'd love.

That is anchoring.

When athletes have an intense emotional experience and can identify and associate a specific stimulus with that experience, they can fire connections between those two things. The stimulus must be repeatedly used to create a strong connection between the feeling and the stimulus.

Here are a few examples.

Motivation for Amateur Runners

Imagine someone trying to get themselves in shape. Despite

knowing that running is an effective solution for weight loss, this person has always perceived running as an oppressive workout and has found it difficult to begin a running routine.

This person sees two sets of grandparents with their grandkids. One set of grandparents has a hard time physically getting around. The other set of grandparents has always been physically fit. Seeing the physically fit grandparents changes the way the new runner sees fitness.

She creates the following mantra: *I'm creating a physically fit future for my kids, my grandkids, and myself.*

Every time she wakes up early to put on her running clothes, she says:

I'm creating a physically fit future for my kids, my grandkids, and myself.

Every time she opens the door to step outside - whether it's raining, freezing, or a beautiful day, she says:

I'm creating a physically fit future for my kids, my grandkids, and myself.

When she comes to the one-mile point, where she typically stops running and begins walking, she says:

I'm creating a physically fit future for my kids, my grandkids, and myself.

When the sweat is pouring down, and she wants to quit, she says:

I'm creating a physically fit future for my kids, my grandkids, and myself.

Her anchor, this mantra, becomes associated with powering through a run. Soon, all she has to do is silently repeat these words to herself. She can trigger the emotional reaction that motivates her into action.

Confidence for Competition

Think of a time during competition when you were confident. A time when you felt powerful. A time when you had not one doubt in your mind. Use your visualization skills to bring every feeling back.

Make a fist. Think more about the confident experience. Make a fist. Repeat again and again.

Give yourself some space - maybe an hour. Test yourself by clenching your fist. If you've anchored effectively, you should feel those same confident emotions coming back.

If you're not there yet, be patient. Continue the anchoring process by visualizing and clenching your fist over and over until the test is successful.

That is how simple anchoring is.

Imagine walking up to the batter's box or the free-throw line and simply clenching your fist to fill yourself with confidence whenever you need it. It can be the difference between winning and losing, and more importantly, between success and failure.

How effective the anchor depends on the intensity of the experience you choose to focus on and the consistency at which it's called upon.

Imagine if you could call up states of motivation and confidence just like that. Consider the possibilities.

What difference could anchoring make in your athletic career? What about in your personal life?

Resourceful State

Many athletes unknowingly walk around with equipment that they have never tapped into. Human beings have natural capacities that can enable them to function at optimal levels and maximize their potential.

The bad news is that most human beings spend too much time operating in a non-resourceful state and end up blocking all of that potential. This non-resourceful state puts us in a rut where we feel like life is a constant struggle, and we might never get to the life we want to have. We work so hard to get to the destination that we don't know how to enjoy the journey.

However, there is good news. The good news is that we can put ourselves into what experts call a resourceful state essentially any time we want. It's like having the ability to flip a switch and transport ourselves to a place where we think more clearly, make better decisions, and live a life that leaves us feeling proud and energetic.

There's even more good news. Getting yourself in a resourceful state is not dependent on circumstances or recent events. You don't have to be performing at your best, winning, or super confident. You don't even have to be on the right track. When it comes to creating a state, you are entirely in control of generating this power. You bring magic to the situation.

Let's clarify. Being in a resourceful state is different from using positive thinking. Being in a resourceful state means changing your mindset so you don't have to convince yourself. You change the way you think so that you know that you can achieve anything, and you feel it throughout your body, heart, and mind. You feel it within every area of your life - your physical life, your emotional life, and your mental life.

You might be thinking that this sounds too good to be true. If it's available and possible, why isn't everyone doing it?

Sadly, the answer is because the old fashioned way of thinking still dominates athletics. Hard work, putting your nose to the grindstone, and slugging through the challenges with nothing more than willpower and stamina are the answers.

Those things are all very worthwhile. But, there is another strategy that will make all of those things so much easier to achieve.

How To Get There

If you're in a bored state, you're going to feel bored.
If you're in a fearful state, you're going to feel afraid.
If you're in a confident state, you're going to feel confident.

Tony Robbins tells the story that when he was 17-years-old, he was living in his car, wondering what the next day would bring. Rather than letting himself remain in a fearful or insecure state, he made radical changes in his physiology and his mental inputs to change his state. He began reading autobiographies about wildly successful people who had overcome similar obstacles. He began training his body because he had learned that fear is physical. Going for a run or lifting weights would automatically diminish fear.

Step 1: Change Your Physiology

There is an acronym ACE, which is helpful to understand.
Action Changes Emotions.
Emotions are difficult to change, or so many think.
Actions are quite a bit easier to control.
Make a radical change in your body, and you make a drastic change in your state.
If you change your state, you change your life.
Try it right now. It's impossible to feel depressed if your body is behaving like it's happy. Go ahead. Try it. Put a smile on your face. Pull your shoulders back. Get up and do ten meaningful jumping jacks. While this is all happening, try to feel depressed. You can't do it.
This is the secret to changing your state.
Let's say it again: Change your state, change your life.

Step 2: Change Your Focus

Give yourself a few minutes at the start of every day to deliberately decide what you will focus on. When you focus and guide your mind, you make it more difficult for the mind to autopilot over to the land of worry and fear.
Need some ideas?

- **Gratitude.** Let's go back to the idea of gratitude again. Focus on finding three specific and unique things about the day for which you are truly grateful. When you focus on gratitude, it's very difficult to experience fear. When you focus on gratitude, it's very difficult to experience jealousy.
- **Intention.** Call upon those new visualization skills. See yourself accomplishing what you are setting out to accomplish for the day.

Post reminders in your car if you need to. Post reminders in your kitchen, your office, whatever it takes to maintain that focus.

By doing this, you will rewire your habits.

Most people want to be happy, but their habits are wired to lead them into feelings of worry, stress, anger, etc. It's like designing a high-speed train to the land of stress and then using a horse-drawn carriage with a broken wheel on a dirt road to get to the land of happiness.

Step 3: Ask Yourself Habitual Questions

On that highway to stress are road signs with questions like:
Why do bad things always happen to me?
What does he have that I don't?
Why is she able to perform so much more consistently than I can?

To change your state, we need to reprogram the inner voice that we all use. One way to do that is by designing and making a habit of asking and answering productive and resourceful-state-centered questions like:
What am I grateful for today?
How many amazing physical gifts have I been given?
What can I do to improve my situation?
How can I take advantage of all the opportunities in front of me?

By asking ourselves questions that set us up for success, we train our minds to work for us rather than against us. We begin dismantling that highway to stress and start paving the road to peace and happiness.

Points to Remember

- Confidence is not about knowing it all or a trait that you have, but something that you work hard to create. Being confident is the certainty that you can accomplish anything you set your mind and energy to.

- By fostering maturity and overcoming insecurity, confidence helps athletes handle relationship conflicts with teammates, trainers, and coaches, and solve problems that arise.
- To become more confident, athletes must change their state.
- Athletes who practice daily conditioning can begin to use positive thinking as a conditioning tool, just like they would a muscle-building supplement.

EPILOGUE

Too many athletes at one point or another in their athletic careers find themselves stuck. They hit a physical plateau in their training, and they can't seem to find a way to improve, or they hit a mental plateau and begin to lose motivation.

When athletes find themselves stuck in this way, they start searching for answers. The critical element in that search is the source.

The internet contains massive amounts of information, but it has become increasingly clear that much of it is worthless because it lacks scientific backing and vetting. It could be a very legitimate program, but it's not right for your particular mental, emotional, or physical makeup. It might not address the underlying issue that is holding you back from pushing through and achieving success.

Some athletes turn to what is commonly being referred to as bro-science. These are techniques or trends that might make an athlete get stronger and look better. Still, upon taking the field to train, practice, or compete, the athlete quickly realizes the effort did nothing for performance. Maybe the extra muscle even makes the athlete feel sluggish and harms performance.

Constructing a plan that will provide real momentum in your athletic career requires you to develop long term strategies that are custom made for you and the particular challenges you face every day in your training and competition.

It can be difficult for athletes to dig deep into the challenges at hand to discover what is getting in the way. Take a step away from all of the big exciting moments in sports - the moments of exhilaration, speed, and accomplishments - to examine yourself as an athlete. Why you do what you do, where you are right now, where you want to go, and how to get there are serious questions. By developing new habits, athletes will uncover these answers and draw insights to unleash potential that they never knew.

Recap

Throughout this book, you have read about the eight habits adopted by numerous professional athletes. Let's quickly recap each of them.

Set Goals and Develop a Plan. Developing a plan helps athletes to build the capacity to focus their energies. By taking the extra few minutes to write down goals, athletes can increase their chances of achieving success.

Stay Consistent and Focused. Being able to focus is one thing. Focusing in the right way and on the right things is another. Successful athletes have realized that consistently engaging in preparatory rituals promote excellent performance. This is critical as athletes need to be able to trust practice and training to take over during competition. When a mistake is made in competition, it is critically important to let it go immediately.

Visualization and Mental Training. What sets apart the athletes who will find real success is mental toughness. When athletes visualize, they purposefully and intentionally rehearse a skill, a routine, or a play in their mind's eye in order and feel the process of creating a successful outcome. They tap into the part of the brain that is later going to perform the actual physical activity. Research proves that the mental activities athletes use to prepare themselves are just as important as the physical elements. When athletes see themselves becoming stronger, faster, and more skilled, the mind helps the body make it happen.

Sleep, Rest, and Recovery. Athletes know that what can be measured can be managed. Coaches must understand the physical and psychological benefits that rest and recovery after training and competition provide. With an increased focus on and an understanding of incorrect perceptions surrounding recovery, athletes can adjust habits and improve performance and overall well-being.

Healthy Eating and Fueling the Body. Athletes often lack specific nutritional knowledge, making it difficult to separate valid information from incorrect information. An athlete's success requires proper nutrition for growth and continued development of muscles, mental function, and the immune system. Nutrition should be the logical application of what athletes know about themselves combined with the basic scientific benefits of food.

Improving Awareness. When athletes develop awareness around their thinking, they open up endless possibilities. Journals are powerful tools of reference that can be used to create awareness and track negative thoughts. Athletes can begin to see their achievements and reflect on how their hard work has paid dividends. They can also identify strategies that work and those that do not.

Building Your Network. For athletes, surrounding themselves with the right people is essential. Having a coach, trainer, or training partner who is willing to seek advice from others, swallow their pride, apologize, and try new strategies is essential. In this chapter, we learned about specialists that can help athletes learn about the brain and how it powers and limits the human body. It gives us the ability to fuel that power and peel back those limits.

Believing in Yourself. Confidence is not about knowing it all or a trait that you have but is something that you work hard to create. Being confident is the certainty that you can accomplish anything you set your mind and energy to. By fostering maturity and overcoming insecurity, confidence helps athletes handle relationship conflicts with teammates, trainers, and coaches, as well as solve problems that arise.

ATHLETE FINANCE

AN ATHLETE'S GUIDE TO FINANCIAL
PLANNING, MANAGING CASH FLOW,
AVOIDING DEBT, SMART INVESTING, AND
RETIREMENT PLANNING

INTRODUCTION

Athletes have many things going on in their lives. They need to manage their training regimen, devote time to healing, and pay special attention to nutrition. In the midst of all this, paying attention to your finances seems impossible. Besides, who has the time to understand those complicated financial terms and conditions?

I'm here to tell you that managing your finances is an essential life skill. Think of it as being as important as swimming or as learning how to interact with other people. It's a basic life skill that is, unfortunately, never prioritized in our education systems. We learn all kinds of useless facts but never learn about essential subjects such as personal finance, taxes, and estate planning.

You might have read other books on personal finance and might have found them difficult to follow. This book is not going to throw complicated jargon at you. Instead, I'm going to break everything down into bite-sized pieces so that you can quickly understand what the deal is with personal finance. It is a deep subject, but do not be intimidated by it. The fact is that most personal finance education isn't geared towards helping common folks understand how their money works.

It's mostly aimed at helping financial advisors promote new products to their clients and better understand new financial rules and

Introduction

regulations. There are exceptions, of course. These exceptions are usually aimed at people with regular jobs who have time left over to devote to analyzing their finances. As an athlete, you don't have the same amount of time.

For starters, you need to train and recover. Recovery is all-important when you're pushing yourself to your physical limit, and your training regimen probably takes up most of your day. Regular people have the luxury of calling it quits from their job at five in the evening, but you don't have this luxury. Does this mean understanding your finances is out of the question?

Hardly. What you need is an easy-to-follow framework that will help you instantly decide whether you're on the right path or whether you need to change a few things up. That's what I'm going to give you in this book. To analyze your finances, you need first to understand what assets and liabilities are. Consider this personal finance 101. Without understanding these basic concepts, it's going to be tough for you to figure out the rest of your money.

Suppose you've tried to educate yourself about money previously. In that case, you might have found that all the solutions and products that are available cause your mind to go into overdrive, and you don't know which ones to pick. Financial advisors do a great job of explaining what a product does to their clients. However, very few of them take the time to explain why that product is a good choice in terms of assets and liabilities.

In this book, I'm going to help you understand how you can easily compare products to one another and determine whether it's a good investment for you or not. If you happen to be flush with cash, you might have friends and family asking you for money. This is especially the case if you grew up in a low-income household. It's great that you can support those around how.

However, you're the one that is earning money, and you have final say over it. You need to treat your money with a certain mindset. In this book, you're going to learn what that mindset is and how you can implement it in your life. I must warn you that this will be uncomfortable at first. However, much like pushing yourself to your limits is challenging and uncomfortable; it's also necessary.

Some athletes find themselves in the unfortunate position of carrying high levels of debt. Debt is a burden that will put the brakes on any of your life's ambitions. Getting rid of it is crucial for success. It doesn't matter whether your debt is small or large. Assuming any debt is dangerous. Not all debt is bad, and this is what confuses people.

Some forms of debt do you a world of good. Learning to distinguish between good and bad debt is one of the many crucial lessons you'll learn in this book. Throughout this book, I've made it a point to keep the language as simple as possible so that you can quickly understand what I'm talking about. You don't need a degree in accounting or a special qualification to figure out what the deal is with your money.

What you need is the desire to understand your money fully and to get your finances in order. Even if you're good with money now, there's a lot you can learn from this book. For example, many people think they're in a good position because they have money invested in a savings account. While this is better than nothing, putting all of your money in a savings account isn't "investing" it.

If all of your money is tied up in a savings account, you're losing money every day. This is just one of the many insights you'll learn while reading this book. I must also mention that some of this advice is going to make you uncomfortable. You might realize you've been doing things incorrectly for a while, and you'll face many questions within yourself.

You might think that your friends and family advise you on one thing, but this book tells you something else. Everyone's natural inclination is to trust those around them the most. However, I can assure you that this book's advice is time tested and is the correct advice. Those around you may have received incorrect information so take the time to educate them as well.

The desire to improve and to achieve a goal is everything. As an athlete, you already know this. While you're used to pushing your mind and body beyond your physical limits, the time has come to tackle an issue that will become bigger later in your life. If you're relatively young

Introduction

right now, you might think you have much time to get your money in order. This is true, but it's the wrong mindset to adopt.

To successfully figure out your money and get it working for you, you need to develop a mindset that prioritizes your money and financial well-being. Without this present, no advice will solve your issues or help you tackle potential ones. So get excited about your money and the fact that you're taking action to figure it out! You're already ahead of most people in this world, not just athletes.

Most people do not have the courage or inclination to understand their finances. They'd rather sweep the problem under the carpet. This isn't you. So pat yourself on the back for taking a great first step! It's now time to move ahead and take another step.

1

ASSETS AND LIABILITIES

The poor and the middle class work for money. The rich have money work for them.

— ROBERT KIYOSAKI

To fully understand money, you need first to figure out what the deal is with assets and liabilities. Here's a simple definition: Assets are things that give you something in return. This could be money, or it could be something such as a good feeling. For example, nutritional supplements can get expensive. However, they help your body recover faster and help you perform better on the field. Despite their high cost, they're assets.

A liability is an object that doesn't give you anything of value. For example, a fancy car is a huge liability. You need to pay an exorbitant amount to purchase it and maintain it. In return, what does it give you? A few cool pics on Instagram, and that's about it. You might get a few admiring looks when you pull up outside a fashionable spot. However, do you need to buy a car to receive these looks? Someone who pulls up in a rental behind you will receive the same looks, and they'll spend a lot less than you.

Many people get confused between assets and liabilities because they think of them as being objects. For example, a fancy car is a liability, and a house is an asset. This is the wrong way to think because a fancy car can become an asset, and a house can become a liability. To better understand the differences between assets and liabilities, we need to look at two important components of your finance equation.

These are cash flow and net worth. Let's tackle cash flow first.

Cash Flow

Cash flow refers to the money you receive every month that allows you to pay your bills, save a certain amount, and invest the rest. Cash in hand is extremely important since you need it to live according to your lifestyle's demands. You pursue your goals on the field or court to generate enough cash to live well. This might not be your primary purpose, but without cash, it's close to impossible to live well. Would you be able to live according to your current situation if you weren't getting paid to do what you do?

There are two components to cash flow. The first is the amount of cash you receive or your cash inflow. The second is your cash outflow, which is the amount of cash you use to pay for your expenses. If your inflow is greater than your outflow, your cash on hand will increase. If it's the opposite, your cash on hand will decrease. The first lesson you need to learn is: Never spend more than your cash inflow.

Active and Passive

Following the principle to never spend more than your cash inflow, we can conclude that it's important for you to maximize it. The greater your cash inflow is, the more money you'll have to spend on the things that satisfy you. You'll have more money to invest and to give to those you care about. For most people, their primary source of cash inflow is their job.

As an athlete, you receive income from the fruits of what you do on your playing field. Your team or sponsor pays you a certain amount of money as a part of your contract. This is similar to a salary that regular folks receive when they work at a nine to five job. In exchange for their effort in the office (field) and their time, they receive compensation.

This source of cash is referred to as being active or time-bound. The amount of cash you receive is strongly linked with the time you spend achieving desired results. For example, your salary is tied to your performance on the field. If you could achieve elite performance without spending time working out, taking care of your mind and body, you would still get paid.

However, as every JV athlete knows, you need to train like the best to be the best. You cannot get away from spending time in practice if you want elite results. Thus, your salary is ultimately linked to the amount of time you spend preparing. Elite athletes, such as those in the NFL or the NBA, get paid millions to do what they love. However, they also spend their entire day training and hire staff to look after their needs. Their time is fully linked to the amount of money they earn.

Active sources of income are great because it's easy to figure out how you can increase the amount you receive from them. For example, you could train better or spend more time working on a skillset and boost your performance. Everyone needs to have an active source of income. The problem is that their nature limits active income sources.

Since they're linked to your time, there's only so much you can earn. You have just 24 hours per day to exchange for money. You need to sleep for at least 10 hours every day to rest and recover. This leaves you with 14 hours to exchange for money. Of these 14 hours, you need to spend at least four to five hours eating and spending time with your loved ones.

This leaves you with nine hours to exchange for money. Everyone's time is limited, and as a result, the income they earn from an active source is also limited. No matter how great your results are, your earnings are limited based on how much time you've spent producing them. If you find that you need to spend more time producing them, you'll have to cut back on other things in your life. You might have to spend 12 hours of training and spend just two hours with your loved ones and on nutrition.

Most people cannot make such sacrifices indefinitely. As an athlete, the number of years you can earn money by playing a sport is limited. There will always be someone younger, faster, and stronger. You can't fight time. Athletes that retire choose other sources of active income. They end up neglecting to develop the second type of cash flow in their lives.

Passive Income

Passive income is tougher to generate than active income, but it's far more rewarding. This type of cash inflow is disconnected from your time spent generating it. You'll need to put the time in upfront to develop the source, but once this is done, it goes away and keeps making you money. The more passive income you have, the greater is the degree of financial freedom in your life.

Imagine living a life where you receive a steady income every month without having to go to work. This is a life that a lot of retirees live, and it's fully possible for you as well. It takes planning and a good understanding of how important passive income is for your cash inflow. Let's say you're receiving a monthly salary of $7,000. This is a pretty good income. Now imagine if someone mailed you a check of $3,000 every month, no questions asked. You didn't have to do anything to produce that income. You simply received it.

That's what passive income is. It allows you to earn money while you sleep. If you have enough passive income, you can do whatever you like with your time and not have to worry about how you'll pay for your living expenses. Sounds great, doesn't it? The catch is that generating enough passive income to pay for your living expenses is tough. Almost every source of passive income involves investing money and earning interest or returns on it.

A savings bank account is a source of passive income. You invest money into it, and you earn around one percent or less as a return every year. Let's say you need to generate $7,000 every month to pay for your expenses and live comfortably. $7,000 per month is $84,000 per year. How much will you need to invest in a savings account to receive this much money every year?

Interest earned every year = Amount invested * interest rate.

Amount invested = Interest earned every year/interest rate = 84,000/0.01 = $8,400,000

You'll need to invest $8.4 million to earn $84,000 per year or $7,000 per month. That's a lot of money! There are other sources of passive income that pay you higher interest rates, but even the best of these will pay you around four to five percent every year. There are ways of boosting your cash return through the use of leverage.

Leverage in financial terms refers to borrowing money. Let's say you wanted to generate $7,000 per month as a passive income from a savings account. You know that you need $8.4 million. Let's say you had just $84,000 to invest (which is also a lot, but this is just an example). What if someone allowed you to borrow $8.4 million on the basis of investing $84,000? They're willing to let you keep $84,000 in interest income and only ask to be paid whatever excess you receive over that Amount every year.

Interest earned = Total investment * interest rate = (8,400,000+84,000)*.01 = 8,484,000*.01 = $84,840

Your desired cash inflow = $84,000

Excess cash received from investment = 84,840-84,000 = $840

Rate of return on your investment = cash you received/ amount you invested = 84,000/84,000 = 100%

This is a pretty sweet deal. It also happens to be beyond unrealistic that anyone would be willing to lend you money like this. However, it goes to show the power of leverage. With $84,000, you can control $8,484,000, and you can turn a one percent interest payment into a 100% gain.

Real estate investments allow you to access leverage, but at far lower rates than the ones cited in the example above. In the above example, you paid $84,000 to control $8,484,000. The $84,000 is called your "equity" in the deal. Think of it as being your piece of the pie.

Equity percentage in a deal = (cash invested / total cash in the deal)*100 = (84,000/8,484,000)*100 = 0.99%

In the above example, you own 0.99% of the overall pie. In a normal real estate deal, you'll own anywhere between three percent to 20% of the pie when starting out. In exchange for giving you money, a lender will charge you interest over a number of years. The lower your equity is, the higher your monthly payment will be. A loan that is drawn against property is called a mortgage.

Mortgages are a perfect example of how debt can be good or bad, and I'll explain this later in this chapter. Let's look at why drawing a mortgage might be a good idea. You can use it to buy a property and place it on rent. Your tenants will pay you rent monthly, and this becomes a source of passive cash flow for you. You'll need to maintain the property and manage it well, but the Amount of money you earn from it isn't tied to the time you spend maintaining it. Carry out preventive maintenance once in a while, and you'll generate the same amount of cash every month.

Real estate investments are a great source of passive income, and this is why many investors flock to it. You will need to go into debt to finance the deal, but as long as you manage it well, this is not a bad thing. Other sources of passive cash flow are business investments. You could invest money in a business that someone else is running, and you could receive a yearly or monthly cash payment.

You could set up an online business that can be fully automated. This will bring you cash flow every month without you having to do anything beyond maintaining the automated processes. The stock market is another source of passive income. Typically, you can earn a return of three to five percent on your investments.

Many retirees use financial instruments called annuities to generate passive income. There are many different kinds of annuities, but all of them require you to invest a lump sum amount with an insurer or a financial firm. You'll receive a certain monthly payment depending on when you want the payments to start and for how long you want to be paid.

Don't get caught up with types of instruments. Understand the difference between passive cash flow and active cash flow. The more passive your cash flow is, the greater is your financial and time freedom. Since passive cash flow requires investment, this will bring you into touch with the second part of your personal finance equation. You've learned about cash flow, and now it's time to look at net worth.

Net Worth

Rich people often talk in terms of net worth. For example, look at the Forbes billionaires list. You'll see that Jeff Bezos, the CEO of Amazon, is "worth" over $100 billion. If the stock market drops, you'll read about how Bezos had "$100 million wiped out" from his wealth. These kinds of proclamations are pure nonsense. This is because the writers of these publications have no clue how money works. Therefore, pay no heed to such sensationalist headlines.

The reason such statements are false is that they refer to Bezos' net worth. Your net worth is the sum of all your assets, minus your liabilities. If you have $100 in cash and $80 in debts, your net worth is $20 (100-80). This is a simple net worth calculation and is a good approximation of how much cash you truly have. However, the type of assets you have can complicate the calculation.

Let's say you own a property (fully paid off) worth $1 million. You have $100 cash in the bank as before and have a credit card debt of $10,000. Your net worth is:

Net worth = Assets - liabilities = Property value + cash - credit card debt = 1,000,000+100-10,000 = $990,100

This paints quite a rosy picture. You're worth close to a million dollars. However, is this a true representation of your cash position? You have just $100 in the bank but are carrying debt worth $10,000. How are you going to pay this bill when it comes due? You can't sell a chunk of your property and use that to pay your bill. Properties don't work like that. Selling a million dollar property to pay a $10,000 credit card bill doesn't seem to be the right thing to do either.

After all, your property could increase in value. It could be worth $2,000,000 in a few years. This example shows how easy it is to get caught up in your net worth and why net worth calculations matter only to a certain point. It would help if you had the cash flow to pay for your living expenses. If you don't have this, it doesn't matter what your net worth is.

What if you have enough cash flow to pay your bills and set aside enough for an emergency but have a low net worth? Is that desirable?

Let's say you earn $7,000 per month, which covers all expenses and leaves you with $4,000 in savings, which you put into a bank account that pays you interest. You don't own property or any kinds of physical assets. Is this a good situation?

While it's much better than the previous situation, it's still not ideal. It would help if you balanced your net worth considerations with your cash flow. Take care of your cash flow above everything else and invest the rest into building assets that boost your net worth. You'll learn how to spot such assets shortly.

A great example of how you can think about net worth versus cash flow comes from the billionaire Warren Buffett. Buffett has been in the top five of Forbes' list since the late 1990s. His net worth has hovered north of $50 billion since that time. Despite this astronomical net worth, he draws a yearly salary of $100,000 from his company. That's how much he needs to pay his bills and have peace of mind regarding cash flow.

As far as Buffett is concerned, the majority of his net worth is just a scorecard. He's an investor, so he uses it to keep tabs on how good his investment decisions are. In terms of paying bills and paying for his daily needs, he couldn't care less about his net worth. Your net worth is important to the extent to which it brings you peace of mind. Let's look at another example that will illustrate the difference.

Let's say you have $1 million in the bank as cash. Another person owns a $1 million property they can live in and has zero cash. Who is better off? The person with cash is. The person with the property still needs to pay bills and maintenance. They have a high net worth but of what use is it? You can't eat a house. Let's now change this up a bit.

The second person now owns the $1 million property and has $500,000 in the bank that they're using to generate passive income to the tune of five percent every year. This means they earn (0.05*500,000) $25,000 every year which is $2,083 every month. What's more, they've placed the $1 million home on rent and are earning $9,000 per month from their tenants.

Their monthly cash flow is (9,000+2,083) $11,083. Over and above this, they work a full-time job, which pays them $8,000 per month.

This brings their overall cash inflow to $19,083. Their expenses are $5,000 per month, which leaves them with a final cash flow of $14,083. They're now using this money to build a business that will bring them even more cash flow.

Compare all of this to the person who has just $1 million in the bank and is doing nothing with it. Who is better off? The second person is. This example illustrates a basic fact about money. Money is worth something only when it's "flowing" from one source to another. It's best if it flows into something that produces more of it instead of flowing into a liability. This is where the first rule of money will help you. Never spend more than your cash inflow, and you'll not have to worry about running out of cash.

Your cash flow can be used to build your net worth, but your net worth is just a scorecard. It doesn't mean anything tangible unless you're using it to generate more cash. This doesn't mean you neglect net worth. It's just that net worth is a result of how well you use your cash. Don't get caught up in net worth calculations and mistake this for wealth. It's paper money. If the stock market falls and Jeff Bezos' net worth dips by $100 million, he isn't losing cash. His paper money has reduced, and he probably doesn't care about it.

Falling into the net worth trap is common amongst many real estate investors. This is because they don't understand what assets and liabilities are.

Assets and Liabilities

How many times have you heard of someone brag about their million-dollar property portfolio or "empire?" Have you read online ads that present some spotty 16-year-old kid as being a property millionaire? I'm highlighting real estate because it's a great example of how misunderstood leverage is. It also highlights how the lines between assets and liabilities can blur into a hot mess if you don't take the time to understand them properly.

Let's begin by defining what an asset is. An asset is something that increases your cash inflow. This deceptively simple definition will save you from a world of pain. Some people think of assets as being investments that increase their net worth. This is false and is a great way of falling into debt traps. Always look at assets as investments that increase your cash inflow. We're not done defining an asset yet.

The second quality an asset must have is maintaining itself and not putting you at risk of falling into a debt hole that will wipe you out. Let's analyze a few investment opportunities to see whether they qualify as assets. The first example is that of a real estate investment.

The property is worth $500,000, and you need to borrow money to buy it. Let's say your equity in the deal is 20%. This means you invest $100,000 and borrow $400,000 from a bank. They ask you to pay a certain amount of cash every month for the next 30 years. Let's assume this monthly payment is $300. You earn $4,000 every month from your job. With me so far? Great!

Your net worth = Assets - liabilities = Property equity - Debt owed = 100,000-400,000 = -$300,000

Monthly cash flow = Cash inflow - cash outflow = 4,000- 300 = $3,700

You now have a choice as to how you want to use this property. You could do what most people do and live in it. This advice is quite common and is presented as being a way to "pay yourself." Are you paying yourself, however? Once you live in this house, your net worth remains the same. However, your cash outflow increases because you'll have to pay for maintenance, utilities, and more. Let's say this amount is $2,000 per month.

Net worth = -$300,000

Monthly cash flow = Cash inflow - cash outflow = 4,000 - (300+2,000) = $1,700

Is this investment an asset? Going back to our two rules for an asset, it doesn't increase your cash inflow. It doesn't pay for itself, and it's put you in a debt hole of $400,000. This debt costs you just $300 per month, which is a very small portion of your monthly cash inflow. However, what happens if you lose your job? How will you pay the mortgage then? Stop making payments, and the bank will foreclose on it, and you'll be out on the street. This house is not an investment.

You can turn it into an investment, however. You decide to place the property on rent and earn $5,000 per month in rent. You'll need to live in a rental property, which costs $2,000 per month, which adds to your cash outflow. What does the equation look like now?

Net worth = -$300,000

Monthly cash flow = Cash inflow - cash outflow = (Salary earned + Rental amount earned) - (Mortgage payment + Rent paid + Maintenance expenses) = (4,000+5,000) - (300+2,000+2,000) = $4,700

Before you bought this property, your cash inflow was equal to your salary, which was $4,000. The property has created expenses, but it's increased your monthly cash flow by $700. It ticks the first box to qualify as an asset. You need to spend $2,000 on monthly rent to live and another $2,000 on maintaining the property, over and above the mortgage expense. This is paid for by the rental money you earn every month. If you were to lose your job, it's not going to put you in a massive debt hold because the rental payment covers all expenses related to the property. It ticks the second box as well. This is a great asset.

As you can see, the same property can behave as an asset or as a liability. If you haven't caught on as yet, a liability is the opposite of an asset. It decreases your monthly cash flow, and it puts you in a debt hole. You turned a liability into an asset by placing the house on rent and deciding to rent your own living space. Can you see why the notion of "paying yourself first" is incorrect? Can you see the number of details that it misses?

I'm not saying it's better to rent versus buy. My point is that you need to calculate your net worth (to figure out your overall debt), your monthly cash flow (to figure out cash inflows versus outflows), and use this to arrive at a full picture.

I'd also like to point out an error that real estate investors fall into. The property in our example was worth $500,000. Many investors assume that just because they control a property worth this amount, they're now worth that much. This is completely false. As long as you have an outstanding mortgage, you don't own anything. You only own equity in the property. This is why the net worth figure is negative.

This isn't a problem, however. If the property is an asset, the rental amount is paying for every expense related to it, so you don't need to worry about falling into a debt hole. As long as you have tenants, you can finance your mortgage, and you won't have to worry about foreclosure.

Contrast this with a real estate "emperor" who claims to be worth $1 million. What they have is $200,000 in equity and $800,000 in mortgages. Their properties might be paid for by the rent, which is great. However, what if the economy tanks and they stop earning rental payments? They're now in a debt hole because they bought too many properties using debt. Bankruptcy is their only option. So much for being "worth" a million.

In the example, we just looked at, what happens if you stop earning rental income on your property? You still have your full-time job ($4,000), allowing you to pay the mortgage ($300). You can still afford to pay your own rental expense ($2,000). Maintenance ($2,000) takes a hit, but you can hopefully keep things at a minimum standard until your next tenant arrives. You're not going to fall into a debt hole or have to declare bankruptcy.

You can use leverage (debt) to boost your net worth, but the more you use, the greater is your risk. As long as you understand that risk and have plans to counter it, you can create an asset. Don't do this, and you'll be creating liability and will require luck to be successful. It's far better to rely on processes and skills instead of luck to be successful. As an athlete, you already know this.

Another Case Study

We've looked at real estate, what about the stock market? The stock market is the other major investment area, so it's worth looking at an example to see whether an investment here is truly an asset. Most stock market investments prioritize net worth boosts over cash flow. Let's say you've invested $10,000 into the market, and this pays you no cash. Its value fluctuates up or down, and that's it.

Since this investment doesn't generate cash inflows, you might be tempted to classify it as a liability (as per the previously stated rules). However, this is not true. You can always sell the investment down the road for a higher price, increasing your cash inflow. Your net worth will be boosted along the way, through the paper gains that your investment realizes.

As far as monthly cash flow is concerned, as long as you're investing money that you can afford, your cash flow isn't impacted. If you're earning $4,000 per month and can invest $1,000 safely, your cash flow isn't impacted negatively. You don't need to spend cash on maintaining the investment; it goes away and behaves as it will. Therefore, this is an asset.

I must point out that a key criterion for something to qualify as an asset is to understand how it works. If you don't understand how it works, you're not creating an asset. I'll explain how to understand best the stock market and real estate investments later in the book. For now, you need to understand what assets and liabilities are.

Can you see why a fancy car is now a liability? It costs you money every month and puts you in a debt hole. How can you turn this into an asset? What if you could lease it to someone to drive for Uber? You'll earn some cash on it, and this reduces your debt burden. You could use it for advertising brands and earning sponsor cash. This will probably allow you to drive it for free (since the sponsor cash will be greater than the monthly payment).

There is a qualitative aspect to an asset you must consider. If you need a vehicle to perform your job well, it's not necessarily a liability. In such cases, you should minimize the negative cash impact. For example, instead of buying a fancy new car, buy an old one for cash. This way, you're not creating a debt burden beyond what is strictly necessary.

Take some time now to think of various examples in your own life. Look at the objects you already own and analyze whether they're assets or liabilities. Is your wallet a liability? How about your clothes? At which point does shopping for expensive clothes go from being an asset to a liability? How about shoes? Watches?

Examine everything. This will train you to think in terms of assets and liabilities. Most importantly, look at your time as an asset. How are you spending it? Spend it training or on the field, and it's an asset.

Spend it with people who drag you down and leech off you, and it's a liability. You don't need to be hardcore and train all the time. Relaxation and entertainment are important, as well. However, realize that too much of something can turn an asset into a liability. Everything is a tool, and it's up to you to create assets as much as possible.

2

MANAGING CASH FLOW

Never take your eyes off the cash flow because it's the life blood of business.

— RICHARD BRANSON

Cash flow is important, and managing it is crucial for your financial situation to remain in a happy place. Managing your cash flow is a tough skill to master. Everyone wants to enjoy the fruits of their labor, so it's natural to want to spend cash on the things you enjoy. If you have someone close to you who needs some cash, it's normal to want to be able to help them out.

Managing cash flow requires some mental skills, as well as some clerical ones. It would help if you looked at the things you want to spend your cash on in the right manner. I'm not saying you need to cut out all forms of enjoyment from your life. Some people think that managing their money means they need to stop having fun. Instead, it would help if you looked at financial discipline as a means of gaining financial freedom.

Without the discipline to practice every day, you cannot be successful on the field. Similarly, without the discipline to manage your money, you cannot hope to get it to work for you. Think of your money as being your best employee. Put this employee to work as much as possible since they'll never tire of it. In fact, not putting it to work is what tires money out.

It would be easy for me to give you a list of budgeting tools and teach you how to manage cash flow, but the fact is that you need to get your head right first. Everything begins with the mind, as you already know. Let's take some time to examine the beliefs and thoughts you have around money.

Your Money Framework

What do you think when you think about money? You've read stories of athletes that earned millions during their playing careers but ended up broke, having to declare bankruptcy. Examples such as LeBron James seem to be rare. James never went to college and earned millions right out of high school. However, he's never been involved in any financial scandal and has never had issues with money throughout his illustrious career. How does he manage it?

While James's specific techniques are unknown, there's no doubt that his mindset regarding money is airtight. He views it as a resource and does not spend it frivolously. While he does buy himself luxuries, he doesn't throw his money away on bad investments or people who aren't worth his time.

James' success with money is proof that it's far more important to possess the right mindset regarding money than it is to receive some special education. It also proves that no matter one's background, it's possible to develop this mindset. James grew up in inner-city poverty and without a father (Kozlowski, 2020). He was thrust into the national spotlight during his freshman year in high school, and despite all of that, he's managed to make his money work for him.

What are some of your beliefs surrounding money?

Money is Bad/Difficult to Make/Evil

Money is a necessary part of our lives, and it happens to be an intensely emotional topic. We learn a lot about money from those around us when we're young. How our parents and caregivers treated money and thought about it defines our deeply embedded beliefs about it. If you grew up in a religious household, you might have heard all about how money corrupts and so on.

We're the product of our innermost beliefs. Is it plausible to think you'd be good at managing money if you believed it was evil? This would be impossible. It's like thinking you're terrible at your sport and still trying to be successful. You can train all you want, but if you don't believe it, you're not going to succeed.

If you spot this particular belief within you, recognize what a huge hurdle it is, and resolve to remove it from your mind. The best way to do this is to install a new belief and to remind yourself of it at all times. Examine how money helps you live a better life. Notice that everything around you comes from the existence of money. How would people eat food without money? How can beautiful buildings and works of art be created without money?

Money is just a tool that allows people to express themselves more freely. If someone used a knife to harm someone, would you turn around and say it was the knife's fault? Money is no more at fault than your shoes are when it comes to creating misfortune or corruption. It's a tool that can be used for good or bad. Use it for good, and it will bring untold prosperity into your life. Use it poorly, and you'll only create harm in your life.

Money Should be Used to...

People have different opinions about what money should be used for. Some people associate money with enjoyment and spend it all on things that bring them the most joy. Others see it as a source of trouble and end up minimizing their spending and don't deal with their money in healthy and financially lucrative ways.

The key is to develop a balance between these viewpoints. While money can be used to bring joy into your life, you need to use it for necessities. As an athlete, your prime is limited, and if you want to maximize your best years, you need to learn how money ought to be used. The answer is quite simple.

The majority of your money should be used to build assets. It's impossible to avoid spending money on liabilities, so it's best to minimize such spending. Do not spend money on liability until you've spent twice that amount on an asset. For example, if you want to spend money buying a fancy watch, have you spent twice that amount on an asset first? Only buy the watch once you've done this.

Awareness of your spending habits is crucial. Look back at your expenses over the past month and make a list of everything that you bought. How many of these were necessities? How many were wants? Wants are the things that you don't strictly need to survive. You need clothes to survive, but do you need that sparkling Armani suit? Ask yourself, why did you buy those things, and what was their utility?

An object's utility goes beyond what you used it for. Did it make you feel good? How long did this feeling last? A house that you've had your eye on for 20 years is going to leave a deeper impression on you than a fancy suit that you saw in passing and felt like buying. The greater the utility of the things you buy, the better your spending is.

Check to see if you're using money to cover up some other perceived shortcomings in your life. People often do this, and it's a great way to convince yourself that money is the root of all evil. This happens because no number of purchases can help you overcome feelings of inadequacy. The more money you spend, the worse you'll feel, and the logical conclusion at that point will be to say that money is what's causing you problems. In reality, it's your unwillingness, to be honest with yourself; that's the issue.

Try to make a list of all the things you believe to be true about money and create positive statements to counter them. For example, if you think you cannot learn how to manage your money, tell yourself that managing money is a skill and that any skill can be learned with enough practice. Read these positive beliefs to yourself every morning once you wake up, and once before you go to bed. Remind yourself of them during every waking moment.

Budgeting

As you start installing positive beliefs around money within yourself, you'll find that the task of budgeting and tracking your expenses becomes a lot easier. If you've never budgeted in your life before this, it's going to be tough. It's a lot like learning to ride a bike. You're going to fall a few times, but once you're done falling, you're unlikely to forget how to do it.

Once you get good with budgeting and tracking your expenses, you'll likely not even need to formally track your spending since you'll develop a feel for how much money you're spending and will spend your cash accordingly. Budgeting is a task that is often mishandled because of how people view it. Budgets are viewed as tools that curtail an individual's freedom. As I mentioned earlier, it's best for you to realize that financial discipline is what sets you free.

A key question that often arises when budgeting is, how should you allocate your money? The best answer to this is to utilize the 50/30/20 budget.

50/30/20

This budget was popularized by Senator Elizabeth Warren and her daughter (Yates, 2017). The premise is quite simple. You spend 50% of your money on your expenses (needs). You spend 30% on wants, and the remaining 20% is placed as savings. The simplicity of this method is what makes it powerful.

Your needs are the things that you have to have to survive and do what you do. Food expenses, transportation, rent, insurance, and basic entertainment are examples of needs. Entertainment might be a head-scratcher. It's hard for most people to view a night out on the town as a "need," even if they'd love to indulge in it.

There's no need for you to cut out your entertainment expenses completely. This is unrealistic and will be detrimental to your mental health. Instead, learn where you need to draw a line. Much like the previous example with clothes, you need some degree of entertainment. You don't need to go around buying everyone drinks at the bar. You don't need to throw lavish parties for those around you. If someone expects you to do this for them because you have money, then it's probably time to cut that person out of your life.

Your wants are the things that bring you happiness in the short term. For example, you could spot a nice pair of shoes that you would like to own. Another example might be buying fancy clothes or a car. Wants feel great, but the satisfaction they bring usually dissipates after a short while. Once the new car smell subsides, you're left with a vehicle that guzzles gas and needs constant maintenance.

Many people end up blowing their money on wants, which is why the 50/30/20 framework is powerful. It gives you clear instructions on how to spend your money. When creating your budget, list all of your needs separately, and list your wants as a single line item. You can even call it "wants." Record all of these expenses here. This will help reinforce that wants are not necessary and that it doesn't matter what the individual item is. As long as it's a want, it isn't all that important.

Lastly, we have investments, which you'll allocate 20% of your income towards. The original framework, as proposed by Senator Warren, includes debt repayment in this category, but this isn't the best way to use your money. Debt repayment is not investing any more than eating medicine for an ailment is one. Much like how the problem with the latter situation is an underlying disease, debt is a problem. Repaying it isn't investing your money in anything. If you had a disease, you'd spare no expense getting rid of it. Your approach to debt should be similar. I'll address this shortly.

Investments include money placed in stocks, real estate, and other assets. Savings accounts are not technically assets, and you'll learn why later in this book. It's always prudent to invest your money in places where it can grow. This is simply putting money to work and to increase the speed with which it flows in your life.

While 50/30/20 is a great way to simplify your spending allocations, it isn't necessary for you to follow these exact proportions. Leaving the world of athletes aside, many people who end up prosperous usually spend less than 40% of their incomes on living expenses. This includes expenditures that can be classified as wants.

This leaves them with 60% of their incomes as savings, and they deploy this money to create more passive income for themselves. Allocating just 20% of your income to savings and investments might work if your income is low. However, as your income increases, it's a good idea to increase that proportion and reduce your spending on wants and needs as much as realistically possible.

The true purpose of investment is to create passive income and assets. You've learned in the previous chapter that doing this takes time and much money. Therefore, it makes sense for you to invest as much as possible, as quickly as possible. You'll learn more about this in the chapter on investment.

Monitor your spending for a month and decide on which proportion makes sense for you. Remember to classify your needs and wants correctly. No one is asking you to give up on your wants. Instead, decrease your degree of spending on them. For example, many people tend to overdo their cheat meals. The correct way to implement a cheat meal is to reduce the amount of food you eat in those meals. Instead of eating an entire pizza, have just a slice. Instead of eating an entire sundae, with Nutella heaped on top, have a scoop of ice cream.

Similarly, don't spend large amounts of money on your wants. Aim to reduce those expenditures by 10% until you can go no lower. If you eat out a lot (no matter how healthy the food might be), cut down this expense by 10% every month. If you spend $200 eating out, aim to spend $180, then $162, and so on. Eventually, you'll reach a stage you'll find it hard to go lower than. This is your optimal level. Awareness and tracking are key.

Tracking Methods

There are two broad ways to track your spending. The first is to track everything in a spreadsheet manually. The second is to use an app. You probably track your calories already in one form or another, so view this as just being an extension of this practice. Manual tracking is straightforward, but it requires you to devote time to performing clerical work.

You'll need to save all of your receipts and enter them accordingly. You'll have to create a pivot table in Excel and track your spending in various categories. Apps make this part of the process easier, but you'll have to spend time classifying expenses. Many apps connect to your bank account and pull expenditures from there directly. As a result, a fancy meal will be categorized as part of your grocery expenses instead of going under entertainment or as a want.

Apps allow you to create your categories, but they don't always support tracking to the most minute detail level. For example, aim to track food expenses by dividing expenses between proteins, carbs, and fat (or rice, protein sources, vegetables, and fat). An app can't do this automatically. It can help you track items only down to the receipt level. You'll need to buy these things separately to automate that level of tracking.

As a result, if you're interested in granular tracking, a manual method works best. If this isn't a concern, use an app. Mint is the best app for financial tracking. It's the oldest app on the market and connects to your bank accounts easily. It also pulls credit card spending and provides reminders for bill payments. There are other apps such as YNAB and Toshl Finance, but Mint is probably the best.

YNAB (You Need A Budget) is best for those carrying a significant amount of debt that needs to be paid off. You'll learn how to approach the question of debt reduction in the next chapter. Make it a habit to start tracking your expenses according to your preferred tracking method. Whatever method you choose, you'll need to spend some time collecting all data together and analyzing it.

Mint provides an easy to understand pie chart that classifies spending according to your categories. You can fix spending limits on each line item, or you can fix an overall limit to your needs, wants, and investments according to your proportion. Fixing an overall limit is probably the better option since some of your line item expenses might spill over. If you wish to go down the line item route, here are the most common expenses you'll have:

- Rent/living costs
- Gym/fitness costs
- Transportation
- Health insurance

- Car insurance (if applicable)
- Food and supplements
- Entertainment
- Cost of support services (mental health, physical recovery etc.)
- Phone and internet
- Utilities
- Grooming
- Miscellaneous
- Education

The most important items on this list are the last two. Miscellaneous expenses give you a bucket to classify expenses that don't fit a particular line item. They also give you a buffer. You may over or underestimate some of your expenses. A bucket that can catch any spills is essential in a budget.

Education in this context refers to investing in yourself. You invest in your body by exercising and training, but how much are you investing in your mind? The easiest way to invest in your mind is to read. Books are the best investments you can make. With the rise of eBooks, you can pay a few dollars to buy great books. Through programs such as Amazon's Kindle, you can rent books for a while without having to pay the full price for the book.

Your playing days won't last forever, so you need to start preparing yourself as early as possible. It's easy to think that you'll always be invincible when you're in your prime, but this is not the case. If you were lucky enough to graduate with a degree, continue to invest in that education. If not, work towards attaining some form of education. It doesn't have to be a college degree. Learn real-world skills such as managing your money (this book is an investment in your education) or programming.

Whichever skill catches your fancy, set aside some time to learn what it takes to develop that skill. You don't need to master it overnight. Perhaps you'd like to start a business after your career is finished. Spend some time networking with people who can show you the ropes.

Perhaps one of your sponsors can teach you this? Get creative and aim to educate yourself. Doing this alone will prevent you from falling into a debt trap or going bankrupt later in life.

Invest in courses that enhance your skills. If you want to learn about real estate investing, you could either pay a successful investor for their time to teach you some of the ropes, or you could take a course online. Suppose computers have fascinated you, but you've never had the time to learn to program. In that case, you can learn online or attend a coding boot camp during your offseason.

A great and free educational resource is YouTube. Every skill on the planet is covered via a YouTube video these days. While you can't learn everything from these videos, you can learn a lot about a topic. You can take various topics out for a test drive before committing to one subject. Doing this goes back to my point in the previous chapter about investing your time. The thing about investing is that all the benefits it gives you compounds. One benefit builds on top of another until the progress you make outstrips the sum of the individual benefits.

Commit to spending at least one hour daily to educating yourself. If you're busy, this is much time. However, find a way to do this. You could watch videos during your meals, or you could spend some time with someone who has the skills you want. Over time, you'll end up building a large body of knowledge that will stand you in good stead.

Take some time right now to figure out how you want to create your budget. What are the line items that apply to you, and how will you track all of them? How will you invest your time, and which metrics can you use to track this? You could measure the results of this time by reviewing the new skills you've learned or viewing how well you're performing certain actions. It's entirely up to you.

What's important is that you take what you've learned in this and the previous chapter and start applying it. Remember the lessons about assets and liabilities? Is the time spent creating a budget and tracking it an asset or a liability? When you need to evaluate your needs versus wants, can you identify wants by viewing them through the perspective of assets and liabilities? Spend some time thinking about all of this, and creating a budget to manage your cash flow will become easy.

3

DEBT

Some debts are fun when you are acquiring them, but none are fun when you set about retiring them.

— OGDEN NASH

What is the easiest way to go broke? Simple! Spend more than what you make and use your credit card to pay for your expenses. While you're at it, borrow money to buy liabilities. As you can see, there's not much that you need to do to push your financial position so deep in a hole that you'll never recover. So what should you do to avoid this situation? That's simple as well!

Avoid doing all of these negatives. Don't spend more than what you earn. Don't use credit cards to pay for your expenses (or use them sparingly and pay them off in full when the bill comes due) and don't borrow money to create a liability. Two of these things involve the use of debt. Credit cards charge you high-interest fees when you don't pay off your balance in full. Debt used to create liabilities was spotlighted in the first chapter when you learned how to evaluate what an asset truly is.

When you're out on the field, do you adopt a warrior-like mindset?

Do you vow to conquer all your obstacles and give it your best, no matter what? This is pretty much the mindset you need to adopt when it comes to debt. Try to make no mistake; debt that pays for liabilities will make it impossible for you ever to be free. Debt is such a serious issue that I will tell you to ignore the 50/30/20 partition that I spoke about in the previous chapter.

In its place, you'll need to use another framework that will help you get rid of your debt as quickly as possible.

Getting Rid of Debt

The advice to ditch the 50/30/20 framework applies to you if you're currently carrying any form of debt. This could be student loan debt, vehicle-related debt, or credit card debt. Mortgages are a tricky subject, and I'll address these shortly. The other kinds of debt you owe have no reason to exist. Student loan debt especially makes no sense, so it's in your best interest to get rid of it as quickly as possible.

Many athletes carry high credit card debt levels because they tend to overspend the minute they start earning money. Your credit card is not a source of free money. Credit cards charge high levels of interest, and if you keep borrowing money at those rates, you're certain to go broke. Vehicle loans are a seemingly normal form of debt to assume, but they don't make any sense once again.

A vehicle's value reduces by up to 25% the minute you leave the dealer's lot. This applies to new cars and used cars, with the latter's values reducing to a lesser degree. A car's value only reduces over time (unless it happens to be a classic, in which case you can't drive it for everyday purposes). Drawing a loan to pay a car is like borrowing money to pay for a restaurant meal. Your food will go bad at some point, so why would you pay the cost of that meal back over a few years?

If you have an outstanding car loan, figure out the remaining amount you owe on it and start planning to save that money up. While you're at it, try to make a list of all the debts you have and order them from the highest interest rate to the lowest. Once this is done, you need to figure out how you will pay off the highest interest debt first.

We don't realize how damaging interest is for our finances. For example, if you use a loan to buy a car that sells for $20,000, at 4.6% interest over a period of five years, you'll pay $365 every month. This is a small amount and easily fits most budgets. However, over the course of five years, you're going to pay $22,020. This is 10% more than what the car sells for. The damage doesn't end there.

Your car's value is going to reduce (depreciate) over that period. It's going to be worth half of what it sold initially at the end of five years. It'll be worth around $10,000 in five years, and you'll pay $22,020 for something that is going to be worth $10,000. Would you give someone two dollars and receive $1 back in return? Of course, you wouldn't. Yet, this is what you're doing when you borrow money to finance a car.

You could turn this equation in your favor by turning your car into an asset. However, if you don't do that, it's one of the worst liabilities you can assume. This example highlights a $20,000 purchase. How much do you think you'd lose buying a Ferrari or another pasta rocket like the big ballers do? Those cars depreciate in the same manner as rock sinks in water. You'll also have to pay maintenance costs, which will be pretty high, close to 10% of the car's sticker price every year.

If you feel the need to drive a fancy car, do the smart thing and get yourself a sponsorship. You'll get paid to drive them around. If you can't land a deal, rent them for a few days, thrash them around, and return them to the rental company. That is what all these cars are good for. Don't be seduced by the pictures of fancy cars.

There are some other purchases that athletes purchase using debt. I'll highlight these for cautionary purposes at the end of this chapter. For now, let's look at how you're going to get rid of debt.

Financial Freedom

The first step to financial freedom is to get rid of debt. This means you need to reduce your spending on your wants to its bare bones. You need to carefully evaluate your needs and reduce your spending on them as much as possible. Even if it means living in situations that aren't quite up to your standard (as long as it's safe), you need to do this. You cannot save or grow your money as long as you have debt.

Pay your highest interest-bearing debt off first. This debt costs you the most, so pay down its principal instead of just making interest payments. Your monthly debt payments have two components: Principal and interest. Principal refers to the amount of money you've borrowed, and interest is the lender's profit. If you pay just the interest and not the principal, you're not making any progress with your debt.

Let's take credit cards as an example. You must have noticed by now that when the payment date comes closer, card companies highlight the minimum payment due? This amount is lesser than the overall balance. The minimum payment is presented as an easy solution for you. Pay far lesser than the amount you owe, and you can keep using your credit card. This is a trick that lenders and banks use to milk you dry.

The minimum payment that is due is just the interest on the amount you owe (the principal). Paying this amount does nothing to reduce your debt. You need to pay off as much of your balance as possible, as quickly as possible. Once you've paid off these balances, cut your credit cards up, and restrict yourself to making just one purchase every month on a card. Pay that off as soon as you get home.

The majority of the money you make must be dedicated to paying down your debt. It makes no sense to save money or invest the money as long as you're carrying debt. The money you save, let's say in a savings account, or even in a stock market investment that grows by eight percent every year, cannot compensate you for the interest you're paying. Your savings are growing at eight percent, but you've borrowed money at 22%. How can you ever expect to make money? 22% is the usual interest rate that credit card companies charge you.

So ignore all the advice about investing for as long as you're carrying debt. Get rid of debt first and then focus on investing in other ventures. If your debt burden is high, consider consolidating all of it into a few payments. You can use the services of debt consolidation advisors. If you have multiple credit lines through credit cards, transfer all of your outstanding debt onto a single card with the lowest interest rate.

Mortgages are the heftiest form of debt you can assume. They last for 30 years, so their ill-effects persist well after your playing days have ended. If you've created a liability using a mortgage, you need to figure out how to extricate yourself from it. Can you place the home on rent? Can you sell the place for a modest profit and get rid of your mortgage debt? Once you sell it, you can buy another property that you can rent and earn cash flow from.

Your property is an asset only if the rental payments cover the costs required to maintain it and the mortgage payment. If you're paying any money out of pocket, then this isn't an asset. If you wish to buy a house for a family member or a loved one, buy it in cash. Don't finance the purchase. If you cannot make payments down the road, not only will you suffer, the person you bought the home will lose as well.

Use an app such as YNAB to track your debt expenses and payments. Pay your principal amounts off as quickly as possible. This makes a huge difference to your monthly interest payments. The lower your principal is, the more your interest payments decrease. Add your debt repayment amount as a line item in your budget and make it a point to pay it every month. It comes before everything except rent/living expenses, food, and water. Minimize your wants and make debt repayment your top priority.

If you find it tough to stay the course, then remind yourself of the mindset you need to possess. I explained this at the start of this chapter. I'm not asking you to cut out entertainment expenses entirely. This would simply be punishing yourself, and that doesn't help anyone. Instead, minimize it. Instead of watching a movie in a theatre, can you watch it at home instead? This doesn't mean you load up on Netflix subscriptions. It means you find cheaper ways of entertainment. You're in no position to drop five figures at the club every night, so don't put yourself in such places.

Once you've paid your way out of debt, you need to focus on staying out of it.

Staying Out of Debt

The best way to stay out of debt is, to be honest with yourself. Are you bad with money, and do you struggle with monitoring your spending? If yes, then lean on someone close to you who can help you manage your finances. Do not outsource financial management to someone else under any circumstances. It's your money, and you should manage it. Lean on them for support and for timely reminders. You're still responsible for your behavior. It's not their job to spend your money for you. They're only present for support.

Switch to the 50/30/20 budget to give your spending a good framework. Your priority, once you've got rid of debt, is to establish a freedom fund. A freedom fund is the same as a rainy day fund, except its purpose is to make you financially free. If you save for rainy days, that's all you'll receive. Save for freedom, and that's what you'll get. This fund should have money equal to six months' to a year's worth of living expenditures.

You must place this money in a savings account to be easily accessible if things go bad for you. Having this money in the bank gives you much freedom since you can accept more investment opportunities and grow your money. You can experiment with different assets thanks to having this amount of money stashed away.

Once this fund is set up, you need to invest in real estate or the stock market. When investing in real estate, remember that you need to create an asset, not a liability. I'll cover investments in more detail in the next chapter. Private investments, such as a friend's venture, also comes under this category. As you focus on building your financial framework, remember these tips to ensure you stay out of debt.

Recognize Your Window

As an athlete, your earning window is a fraction of the size of a regular person's. A person who works at an office can retain their position for close to 30 or 40 years. The average athlete has a window of 10 years, less in the case of physically demanding sports. The money you make in 10 years needs to last you for close to 50 years. In a regular person, they need to make money they earn over 40 years last for 20 to 30.

Given this reality, you need to make good financial decisions. Try not to rush into any decision without understanding everything about it. Don't get swept in the rush of having to grow your money as quickly as possible. Instead, follow the framework you've learned and keep stashing your money away for your future.

Educate Yourself

Your financial education doesn't end with this book. This is just the beginning. Make it a point to study finance and money as much as possible. Remember your education fund? That's what this is for. Read books and listen to people who know what they're talking about. Unless your childhood friend has a financial degree or has made much money by themselves, try not to listen to them.

Learn how to invest wisely. The next chapter's material is a good starting point but doesn't think that you're done once you read it. Education is a continuous process, and the more you learn, the better off you'll be. You'll have many people tugging at your wallet, so you need the education to protect you from losing all of your money.

Rein in Your Spending

Why do athletes go broke? Examine the case of pretty much any former athlete, and you'll see that all of them end up spending money on things that make no sense. For example, Allen Iverson, who earned more than $200 million during his time in the NBA, was forced to file bankruptcy because he couldn't pay an $860,000 bill for jewelry. There are two remarkable stats here. First, Iverson could not pay a bill that was just 0.43% of his total career earnings.

Second, he was spending six figures on jewelry despite knowing he could not pay the bill. He might not have known the extent of his poverty, but he certainly must have known that his money was running out. Jewelry is a particularly problematic expense since many people have false conceptions of it. I'll explain why this is at the end of this chapter when I list the worst purchases you can make with debt (or with cash).

If you feel the need to rock some bling, remember that it's better to be rich than to look rich. Have you ever seen Bill Gates wear any bling or even drive a fancy car? Gates is what real wealth looks like. The average rapper rocking his bling is what "broke in 10 years" looks like. Decide whom you want to be.

Keep Good Company

What's the best way to stay out of trouble? The answer's obvious: don't go anywhere near it. Much like how Alcoholics Anonymous members stay away from bars and places that serve alcohol, you need to stay away from people and places that could potentially spell trouble. LeBron James might come across as extremely self-absorbed, but when have you ever read stories of him being in the middle of trouble at a club or having to appear in court because he was an accomplice to illegal activity?

I've already highlighted James' tough upbringing, so it's not a question of growing up in the wrong neighborhood. All that matters are your priorities. If you choose to stick with people who constantly get into and out of trouble, it's a matter of time before you're going to get dragged into it. Keep your circle close, and do not let anyone manipulate you into spending your money.

If you're unsure of whether you're spending your money the right way, use professional help and seek their advice. Going back to LeBron James' example, you might look at how he hired his friends to manage and build his empire. However, his manager and close friend Maverick Carter has always said that it wasn't about giving friends and family a free ride. Everyone on the team had to bring skills to the table. Without it, there was no point in giving them access to James' money.

Cater has also spoken about how James and his team used the example of Jay-Z as a model of wealth-building (Rhoden, 2018). It wasn't about earning money for James. It was about building assets that would outlast his playing career. The way he did was by focusing on becoming the best basketball player he could be while having his trusted team look after his business interests. You don't need to reinvent the wheel. Just copy this model and reap the benefits for yourself.

Purchases to Avoid

There are a few types of purchases that every athlete seems to make no matter which sport they're from. Some of these purchases are emotionally driven, while others arise due to a lack of education. Some of them are fueled by debt, while others are bought with cash. This doesn't make their negative impact any lesser. To stay out of debt, you need to tread carefully around these purchases. Not all of them are bad or death sentences. However, they contain pitfalls that you should be aware of before investing.

Jewelry

Blame pop culture and a lack of education for this one. It isn't just athletes but even regular folks who buy jewelry with the aim of "investing" their money. Gaudy chains, rings, bracelets, and watches are like fast food. They taste great in the here and now, but once you're done eating them, you'll feel terrible.

Precious metals are a good investment. Gold, silver, and other metals such as platinum and palladium have proved to be excellent preservers of wealth. Gold has always been a way for the wealthy to preserve their net worth. However, jewelry is not the same as precious metals. This is because each piece of jewelry is customized. Unless you happen to be subject to some very peculiar circumstances, your jewelry will not worth anything.

Diamonds are probably the most overrated form of expense. They have no utility beyond a few industrial applications and behave much like cars do when it comes to their value. Their supply is kept artificially low, and jewelers convince saps to spend three months' income on engagement rings. They shine a lot, which doesn't hurt their appeal. However, your diamonds are worth nothing on the second-hand market. Unlike other forms of jewelry, they can't be melted and turned into something else. Silver and gold jewelry hold their value to a large extent because of this. However, you might as well toss a diamond into a garbage can once you buy it.

This is not to say they're completely worthless. However, they're not as valuable as wealth preservers, as most people believe. A diamond engagement ring is undoubtedly one of the worst ways of using your money.

Cars and Mansions

While most people are smart enough to use cash to buy jewelry, they draw loans to pay for cars and mansions. The reasons for cars being a terrible investment has already been outlined. As for mansions, you've learned how you can create liability by drawing a mortgage. Make sure you fully understand the numbers behind a real estate investment before you sink money into it. Real estate investing involves the use of leverage. This boosts your gains significantly, but it can also sink you if mismanaged.

There are many creative ways of structuring leverage to boost your investment return. However, all of these are risky if you don't understand how they work. For example, you can draw what is called interest-only mortgages that have extremely low monthly payments. The idea is that you finance the property with this mortgage for four years, earn rental income that far outstrips the mortgage payment, and sells the property for a higher value in four years. Why four years? Because the principal kicks in after this period and monthly payments balloon. If mismanaged, this balloon can bankrupt you.

Business Franchises

These can be excellent investments. However, not every business franchise is worth buying. A lot goes into making a successful franchise, and often, even successful businesses in one part of the country struggle to replicate their success elsewhere. For example, just because Papa Johns does well in Denver, this doesn't mean it'll be a hit in New York.

Many athletes invest in businesses they frequent, and this can be a potential mistake as well. Investing should be carried out rationally. Just because you happen to like the pizza at a local pizzeria doesn't mean everyone else will. You need to consider the numbers presented to you and take several other factors into account. I'll cover these in the next chapter.

For now, resist the temptation of investing in a friend's business just because they're close to you. Do not invest in coffee shops, upscale restaurants, nightclubs, and other "cool" businesses. What do I mean by this? If you're buying a business because you think it would be cool to own it, it's probably going to be a bad investment. No one brags about owning a few Subway franchises or a few Krispy Kreme locations. These are boring businesses, but they're precisely the ones that make you money.

Fancy Products

Athletes attract all kinds of people, and there's always someone who has an idea for the next path-breaking invention. These inventions usually break bank accounts, not paths. It's exceptionally hard for someone to launch a new product on the market. Even Steve Jobs got it wrong with some of his investments. The man who invented the iPhone and other jaw-dropping devices was also an investor in the Segway, which was named one of the worst inventions ever (Fletcher, 2010).

Stay away from inventions and new product launches unless you happen to know the market intimately. Even then, it can be tough to get it right. If you want to take a risk, place a small percentage of your investment funds into such an invention. I'm talking less than one percent of your total investment capital. That way, if it does come off, you'll make a massive profit. If it doesn't, you haven't lost much.

4

INVESTMENTS

It's not how much money you make, but how much money you keep, how hard it works for you, and how many generations you keep it for.

— ROBERT KIYOSAKI

Investing your money can be intimidating. There are many options out there, and there are many examples of investments failing. For every instance of someone like Shaq owning 155 Five Guys restaurants, there's Raghib Ismail losing everything on an investment in a Rock n' Roll Cafe.

In this chapter, you're going to learn about the various investment choices you have and how you can make sense of them. There is a common thread that connects every investment evaluation. This is to do with how you evaluate risk. Risk is ever-present, and it's easy to forget how damaging it can be. What is a risk when it comes to investment?

Risk is the probability of you losing all of your money. That's what it comes down to. You can reduce the probability of losing money by educating yourself. This allows you to understand the opportunity fully and evaluate your expected rate of return. Do not get caught up with the potential rewards and neglect risk. For example, let's say you want to open a gamer's cafe. You could look at the rise of esports and gaming in popular culture and decide that there's money to be made there.

Despite the huge potential, you still need to look at the negatives that bring risk to the table. What if your cafe is in a bad location? What if gamers decide to play online and not in physical cafes? What if you can't maintain your locations well enough to entice gamers to keep coming back? Many things contribute to an investment opportunity's risk.

Chief among these is your ability to make the investment work. Many investments are bad choices not because their business models are bad, but because their owners are incapable of executing them. When it comes to your investments, leave the "tough it out" mentality behind you, or on the field. Investment success comes from sticking to what you know and can realistically execute.

You could own a chain of restaurants, but do you have the time to manage the business? Do you have the time to run the books and figure out how each restaurant is doing and whether some are increasingly making losses? If you don't have the time to do this, do you know someone who can run these numbers for you? What will their services cost, and how much do you trust them?

Many athletes don't ask themselves these questions and end up squandering their cash. It would be best if you looked at risk in other dimensions as well. Have you ever noticed that most athletes only seem to place their money in private businesses such as restaurants, cafes, and bakeries? They never seem to brag about their stock market investments. This is because the stock market is completely misunderstood, and it scares away most people.

This is a tragedy because the stock market can make you a lot more money than a private business can. Even better, it can increase your cash flow. A private business only increases your net worth unless it happens to be an already established business. For example, Andre Igoudala has invested a ton of money into private technology companies worth over a billion. These are good investments.

However, they don't add to his cash flow. If he wants to sell his shares, he's not going to get anywhere near what those companies are said to be worth. This is because he'll have to sell it to other company insiders who will squeeze him on the price. It's impossible to know what his financial situation is like. However, if he's taken care of his cash flow needs, these net worth boosting investments are good decisions. If not, he's going to land himself in trouble.

The primary aim of your investments should be to create passive income for yourself. Passive income benefits have been outlined in the first chapter. If you're still not sure of why this is great, please read the first chapter again. Your goal should be to have the majority of your living expenses paid by your passive income. Once you reach this point, you'll be truly free since you won't have to rely on your regular paycheck anymore.

With the goal of passive income generation in mind, let's look at some of the best ways to generate it, with the best options listed first. Despite some of these options being better than others, don't feel as if you "have" to be invested in all of these options. Ultimately, the risk is lowest when you understand the investment. If you don't understand a particular investment method, feel free to stay away from it, and educate yourself as to how it works before opting for it.

Real Estate

Real estate is a great option for many athletes because you won't have many problems qualifying for financing. Financing approval is what trips up regular folks and prevents them from accessing great real estate opportunities. There are a few things to keep in mind when it comes to real estate. Think of these as the basics.

Types of Properties

Broadly speaking, you will find residential and commercial properties. Residential properties are where people live, and commercial properties are where they shop and where companies conduct business. When it comes to investing, it's safest to start in residential properties. This is because there's always a demand for housing, and it's easier to evaluate your tenants. Banks love residential properties for the same reasons, and you won't have issues getting a mortgage.

Should you use a mortgage or buy in cash? This is a good question to consider. If you're in the prime of your career, then it's best to use a mortgage since you can boost your returns massively. While you're in your prime, you have cash coming in, and you should use as much of this cash to invest and grow your wealth. Buying properties with cash eliminates debt risk, but your wealth will grow at a slower pace.

For example, let's say you have your eye on a $100,000 property. If you finance this purchase, you can control the property with $20,000 upfront. If you had to invest $100,000, are you better off investing it across five financed properties adding up to a total of $500,000 or just one property worth $100,000? If you're in your prime and expect to earn money for the next five years or so, the former is a better choice. If you're nearing the end of your career, you want to minimize risk and avoid debt as much as possible. The latter will be a better option for you.

It comes down to how safe your cash flow is. If you feel it's unsafe, then buy with cash. Coming back to residential properties, you can buy single-family or multifamily properties. These indicate how many families live on the property. A single-family home is your typical property in suburbia. In contrast, multifamily properties are multiple units housed within a single structure. Note that apartment blocks are considered commercial properties.

A single-family home can be partitioned and rented out to multiple people. For example, most off-campus housing on college campuses is this kind of property. These properties make for great investments since there will always be a demand for housing from college kids, and you can boost your investment return by renting individual bedrooms instead of the entire home.

Financing

There are a few important terms you need to learn with regards to real estate financing. The first is a down payment. This is the money you pay upfront to the lender to buy the property. The down payment is your equity (remember this from the first chapter?) in the property.

Usually, banks will require you to put 20% of the property's value down. They'll loan you 80% of the property's value.

The next term to learn is closing costs. Closing costs are fees you will pay to the various professionals that assist you in completing your purchase. There's a lot that goes on in the background, and these people need to be paid. These costs usually amount to three percent of the property's value. If you buy a property in cash, you'll still need to pay closing costs.

The financing approval process takes anywhere from a month to three months. It gets delayed because banks ask for a ton of documents, and it takes time to procure them if you haven't prepared ahead of time. The best thing to do is speak to a real estate agent who can give you a high-level overview of what will be necessary. Prepare these documents ahead of time and apply for pre-approval. Pre-approval is a bare-bones version of the final approval process, and it speeds up your application when the time will come.

Besides traditional banks, you can apply for Federal Housing Authority (FHA) loans through approved lenders. FHA loans require lower down payments, to the tune of three percent or 10 percent depending on your credit score. However, you will need to live in the property if you wish to use these loans. Carefully consider whether you can monetize such property before opting for it. It's also a good idea to pay more down and build equity when buying a property.

This reduces your monthly mortgage payment and makes it easier for your rental payments to cover all costs. You'll create a better asset. Paying more down also gives you the option of reducing your payment term. Instead of opting for the traditional 30 years, you can aim to pay your property off in 20 years or 15 years if you can manage it. Don't go for the biggest or shiniest home. I'll talk about evaluating properties shortly.

You'll have additional expenses to take care of, such as property insurance (flood, fire, and liability) and property taxes. Taxes are a small percentage of the overall value of the property. However, many people are unaware of how critical they are. They're usually just 1.1% of the home's value, but if you neglect to pay them, you can lose your property. Imagine losing a $200,000 property because you forgot to pay a $2,200 bill at the end of the year! Never forget your taxes. If you don't pay them, the county will auction called a tax lien on your property. A lien is a document that indicates someone has a claim on your property due to unpaid debt. Unpaid taxes are owed to the government, and they come ahead of the mortgage on the property.

This means the government technically has the first claim on your property in case of a payment default (tax payment default). The bank has the next claim (if you have an unpaid balance on your mortgage), and only then do you have a claim to your property. The next time you hear someone talk about how they "own" a million-dollar property, ask them if they have a mortgage and if they've paid their taxes on it.

As long as you have a mortgage on a property, you don't own it. The bank owns it. You have their permission to use it and monetize it. Never forget this. Many real estate investors walk around thinking their property's value can be added to their net worth. This is false. Their equity in the property can be added to their net worth, not the entire value if they have an outstanding mortgage.

You should try to understand this since many investors borrow large sums of cash (draw many mortgages with banks) and think that they're home free since the rental income covers the mortgage payment. This is the case when times are good. What happens when times get rough, and their tenants start losing their jobs? Rental payments dry up, and all of a sudden, their mortgage payments are too much. Bankruptcy and foreclosure are the only way out. It isn't just athletes who fall prey to this; smart real estate investors do so as well. Donald Trump's many bankruptcies resulted from his borrowing too much money and not being able to make payments when the rental income dried up.

So how can you protect yourself? This is where property evaluation plays an important role.

Evaluating Your Investment

The first step to evaluating a property is to ask whether it passes the one percent rule. This rule states that the monthly rental income must be at least one percent of the property's value. For example, if the property is worth $200,000, the monthly rental you can earn must be at least $2,000. Anything below this is not worth it.

Next, you need to estimate costs. Maintenance, utilities, taxes, and vacancies are all costs. Vacancies are an insidious cost since no one considers that their property could lie vacant for extended periods. How can you take all of these costs into account? Simple! Assume that your costs are going to be half of your rental income. If you earn $2,000 in rent, you're going to pay $1,000 per month in costs.

You won't pay this amount every month, but over time, this is what it will average out to. To ensure that this is a reasonable estimate, you need to evaluate the property's qualitative aspects. Location, proximity to urban centers, schools, crime, and neighborhood classification are important factors to consider. It's best to work with a smart agent who can bring you properties that satisfy these criteria. You can even invest in properties that already have tenants in them. These are called turnkey rental properties and provide you with cash flow from the first day.

Educate yourself with regards to evaluating a property. The best resource for this is The Book on Rental Property Investing by Brandon Turner. Turner runs a real estate investment website called Bigger-Pockets that covers the world of real estate. His book dives into many different forms of rental investing that won't apply to you. Please focus on the chapters where he talks about evaluating properties and the problems to watch out for. Please do not invest in properties until you've read his book. I would detail how to evaluate property locations as well, but it would take me the rest of this book to do so. There are other pressing issues we need to discuss!

Stock Markets

Stock market investing is the second major wealth generator for you. Like real estate investing, it is intimidating and seemingly controlled by big Wall Street banks. This is laughably untrue. The big banks have no more of an idea of what the market will do than you do. The billionaire investor Warren Buffett has regularly said that he has no clue what the market will do tomorrow or over the next decade.

So how can you make money? Making money in the stock market is deceptively simple. All it takes is for you to follow a few simple principles. While they're easy to understand, following them is hard because of how the financial media covers the markets. They focus on the short term and make it seem as if the markets are either rocketing up or spiraling down all the time. They make ludicrous statements such as "Jeff Bezos lost one billion dollars yesterday. Here's how you can "protect yourself" and so on. I've already detailed why this state is false in the first chapter.

Here are some simple principles for you to remember when investing in the stock market:

1. The stock market is simple. Financial institutions make it complex. Ignore them.
2. Minimize your costs of investment. Costs include taxes, inflation (I'll explain this shortly), and commissions.
3. Set and forget your investments. The only exception is if you have a good knowledge of accounting principles and desire to learn all about them to make better investments. Even then, invest passively.
4. Invest in opportunities where you'll keep your money for at least a decade. Anything under a decade is meaningless to you.
5. Invest in instruments you understand. If you cannot understand it, do not invest, no matter how much money you can potentially make or how stupid someone thinks you are.
6. Do not fool yourself. Be honest about your abilities. Avoid stupidity instead of trying to be clever.

These principles are the same as those that Buffett and a host of other famous investors such as Bill Ackman and Ray Dalio have espoused. They're active investors, but you'll see that it applies to pretty much any form of investing if you read these principles again. Point 4 might not always apply to an active investor. However, you aim to set and forget your investments. You don't want to lose sleep or get distracted by them.

Here is the easiest strategy to follow.

Index Investing

An index is a collection of stocks that have something in common with them. Indexes are created by large financial corporations such as Standard and Poors and Moodys. If you've read anything about the stock market, you will have come across the S&P 500. This is an index that approximates overall market performance. It consists of the 500 biggest companies in America and tracks their performance. Each stock's performance to the index is added, giving the index a value that can be tracked.

Here's a simple example. Let's say you have a three stock index. Each of these stocks is priced at $10, $20, and $50. Add these up, and you have an index value of $80. Let's say tomorrow; these stocks sell for $5, $30, and $40. The index value is $75. The S&P 500's calculation is complex, but this is the essence of it. You do not have to figure out how the index is calculated. What's important is for you to recognize the power of an index.

The S&P 500 used to look very different back in 1926 when it was first established. Back then, railroads and heavy manufacturing companies dominated it. In the 1950s, the railroads steadily vanished as manufacturing and chemical companies dominated it. By the 1970s, the manufacturing companies began faltering, and banks took their place. By the 1990s, manufacturing companies vanished, and financial firms dominated the index and fledgling technology companies. Today, the index is dominated by technology companies such as Apple, Google, and Amazon.

What's the lesson here? Despite the individual sectors facing ups and downs over the past century, the S&P 500 has always managed to capture the best-performing companies. This is because its criteria are simple. The 500 biggest companies get in, irrespective of which industry they're active in. This has resulted in the index gaining an average of 10% every year since its inception. It hasn't risen by this amount like clockwork, but this is the average performance.

The lesson here is that instead of predicting what the fortunes of individual companies might be, it's better to bet on the broader stock market index. America's economic position is strong enough that its companies will remain at the forefront of the industrial revolution for the foreseeable future. Despite China's rise and occasional news about how pretenders like India and Brazil are rising, America's dominance remains unquestioned.

This means all you need to do is invest in the index, and your money will grow over time. The problem is that you cannot buy an index. It isn't a tradable instrument. However, you can buy funds that track indexes.

Index Funds and Exchange Traded Funds

An index fund is an instrument that is run by a fund manager. The manager buys all the stocks present in an index and aims to track the index's performance. For example, you can buy an index fund that tracks the S&P 500. By doing this, you'll closely replicate the index's performance in your portfolio. All you'll need to do is make one purchase to buy units of the index fund.

The S&P 500 isn't the only index you can track. Other indexes include those that track foreign stock markets, real estate markets, bond markets, and dividend-paying stocks. Investing in dividend-paying stocks' indexes makes the most sense, from the standpoint of investment simplicity.

A dividend is a cash distribution that a company makes to its shareholders. They usually pay a sum of cash that will amount to a maximum of five to six percent of the stock's price. This is called the yield. For example, if a company's stock is selling for $100 and pays a $4 dividend, it's yielding four percent (4/100). Higher yields are attainable, to the tune of 15% and above. The problem is that declining stock prices usually cause higher yields.

From the previous example, if the company paid $4 the previous year and if its stock price declines to $50, its current yield will be (4/50) eight percent. This looks great on paper, but a declining stock price produces it. This is not good news for investors. It indicates there's something wrong with the company and that their money might not be safe. It's far better to focus on investing in index funds that track dividend-paying stock indexes.

Two major indexes track dividends you should pay attention to. The first is the Dividend Aristocrats index. This index screens stocks that have paid a dividend for at least 25 years. Not only should these companies have paid a dividend for this time, but they also need to have increased their payouts consistently. These companies are extremely safe and will probably be around forever. Even if they don't, the index will screen in the new top-performing companies. Businesses such as Coca Cola, Johnson & Johnson, and P&G are a part of this index.

The second index is the Dividend Achievers index. This index's criteria are the same, except the period of dividend payment and increases are ten years, not 25. This index captures more growth-oriented companies since the period is low. You can buy index funds that track this index as well.

By buying an index fund, you'll make just one purchase that will give you exposure to an entire world of dividend-paying stocks. The reason dividends are powerful is because you get paid cash for your investment. A typical dividend index fund yields two percent. This means you're going to earn at least two percent on your investment every year. This is your cash flow. Your net worth will be boosted by how much ever the price increases every year.

Prices are not guaranteed to increase every year, and this is why it's important to remain invested for a long period. You cannot hope to earn the average 10% gain in the index over a period of five years or so. Aim to remain invested for over 15 years and do not withdraw this money under any circumstances.

Keep contributing to this account regularly, and your money will grow over time. How much can you grow it to over 20 years? Let's use the calculator at http://www.moneychimp.com/calculator/

compound_interest_calculator.htm to figure this out. Let's assume you invest $12,000 in the first year. This is equal to $1,000 per month, which is attainable if you're fiscally prudent, as described previously.

You will contribute this amount every year for 20 years, and your investment will grow at an average of 10% during this time, every year. How much will you be left with? Plugging these numbers into the calculator, we see that our ending principal will be $768,029. What happens if you remain invested for 25 years? you'll have $1,310,181.

If you live on 40% of your income and save 60% of it, you can contribute a lot more than $1,000 per month. Let's say you earn $5,000 per month after taxes and live on $3,000 per month. This results in you saving 40% of your income, which is $2,000. If you contribute this amount to your investment account, how much will you have at the end of 25 years? The answer is $2,620,362.

Your objective should be to generate enough passive income from your prime earning days so that most of your investment contribution will come from this. Let's say you buy a property in cash and invest the rental proceeds in the stock market. You continue to live off your active income. Once your playing days are over, you can work a regular job that pays most of your bills, and your passive income covers the gap. Your investment contributions can continue, even if they're reduced.

By the age of 60 or 65, you'll have more than a million dollars in your investment account. I'll discuss how to live off this income in the next chapter, where I'll discuss retirement options. Index fund investing will get you to this level easily. Index funds aren't the only investment option you have.

Exchange-traded funds or ETFs are also managed funds. The difference is that ETF prices move during the day, unlike index fund prices, and they don't have investment minimums. The typical index fund has investment minimums of $3,000. This is not the case with ETFs. You can buy ETFs that employ an index tracking strategy. You can get adventurous with ETFs but avoid the complex ones.

Coming back to dividend investing, you have the option of reinvesting your dividends into your investments. This is called a Dividend reinvestment Program or DRIP. DRIPs can boost your investment gains massively. In the previous scenario, we assumed that your investment would grow at 10% per year. This gain is achieved through increases in the price of the index fund or the ETF. This is called a capital gain. Dividends are cash-flow gains. They put two percent (in the case of most ETFs and index funds) in your pocket every year. You can reinvest this two percent and grow the amount of principal you're investing every year for free.

ETFs and index funds charge fees for the services they provide. Do not pay more than 0.05% of your principal as fees every year. Some of the most reputable ETF issues, such as Vanguard and iShares, charge around 0.02% of your principal as fees. This is an extremely reasonable fee to pay.

Investment Accounts

When investing in the stock market, you have two options. You can invest through a retirement account or a normal account. Most professional sports leagues in America offer what is called a 401(k) retirement account. Under the terms of this account, you can direct a portion of your pre-tax income to an investment of your choice. Best of all, your employer (the league) will match this contribution up to a certain percentage.

For example, let's say you're earning $100,000 per year before taxes. This is roughly $8,333 per month. You can divert $2,000 per month to an investment account containing your ETF or index fund holdings. Your employer will usually match 40% of this amount and will deposit the money into your account. This means you'll receive $800 per month for free.

I'll cover retirement accounts in more depth in the next chapter. For now, understand that you won't pay taxes on your gains or dividends until you withdraw the money at the age of 60. It would help if you tried to collect as much free money from your employer as you can through matching contributions. Make it your aim to contribute so much to your retirement account that your employer will feel the need to pull you aside and tell you to take it easy! They're legally obliged to match a percentage of your contributions, so it's not as if they can stop you from doing it.

Retirement accounts have contribution limits, so you'll need to open a regular investment account with a broker. Brokers offer many different accounts, namely, cash accounts, margin accounts, options trading accounts, and commodity investment accounts. Opt for a cash account. You don't need any of the other stuff to invest successfully.

You'll have to pay taxes on your gains, and I'll cover this topic two chapters from now. Taxation isn't too complicated, so don't worry about this too much. Your broker will provide you with all the forms you need. Many brokers these days offer zero commission trades, so you don't have to worry about paying high commissions. If you happen to trade regularly (multiple times every day), then you'll pay commissions. However, as you've learned already, all you need to do is invest a lump sum every month and leave it at that.

Opening a brokerage account is straightforward. You can choose an app such as Robinhood or a full-service brokerage such as Charles Schwab. Discount brokers such as Firstrade also offer you all the necessary services. When picking a broker, make sure they're registered with the Financial Services Authority (FINRA).

That's all there is to stock market investing. As you can see, it's extremely simple and automatic. People love to overcomplicate things, and this is why they lose money. Don't worry about what the market is doing in the short term. Let the financial news scream about how bad things are. Your objective is to remain invested over a period of 20 years or more. Start as quickly as you can and remain invested for a long as possible.

I must state that it's important for you to get rid of debt and establish your financial freedom fund before investing in the market. The objective of this investment is not to touch the money until you're retired. Without these prerequisites, you'll be likely to withdraw your money, and this will hurt its growth. Avoid this as much as possible. This is why you should invest money that you will not miss. This way, there's very little chance of you having to withdraw this money.

Please do not invest in the stock market with the intention of having it pay for your property's down payment or any other expense. The stock market isn't a lottery ticket, so don't treat it this way. Follow the sound investment principles that I've outlined in this chapter, and you'll be just fine.

Gold, Silver and so on

Precious metals can be good investments but don't invest the majority of your portfolio into them. It's best to invest five percent of your portfolio into gold ETFs and leave it at that. The same applies to cryptocurrencies as well. Remember that your investment in these alternative assets shouldn't exceed more than 10% of your overall portfolio, with five percent being optimal.

This is because these assets fluctuate a lot. They're also not backed by anything real like stocks are. A stock represents a business that has office space, employees, earnings, customers, and inventory. Cryptocurrency has nothing backing it other than the feelings of many people. As long as the feeling persists, their values remain high. Once the bubble pops, it's all worthless. The same applies to gold as well. You can debate till kingdom come about how long the feeling that drives these assets' values will last. However, the point is that feelings are not tangible things. You can't invest based on feelings, so avoid or minimize this.

As for other commodities such as oil or agricultural products, stay well away from them. These are intensely speculative assets, and they fluctuate a lot. You're best served to avoid stupidity, instead of trying to be too smart. Recall this is one of the primary rules of successful investing. Stay within the bounds of what you know, and you'll be successful. Let other people experiment with their money. Your objective is to be as boring as possible. This is what will help you sleep well at night.

Private Businesses

Private business investments should be last on your order of priorities. This is because they're extremely hard to extricate yourself from in case things go wrong. Let's say your real estate investment goes wrong, and you want to get out of it. You can place your property on the market and receive offers for it within a reasonable period. If a stock market investment goes bad or if you want to withdraw your money, all you need to do is click a button. You'll get your money back, even if it isn't the amount you invested.

With private businesses, you don't have such options. Your business is not traded on the stock exchange, and it's hard to convince regular people to buy your shares in the business. You'll most probably have to sell them to other business people who will squeeze you on the price. There's also the fact that a business is not an easy thing to execute. The majority of businesses fail because of how hard it is.

No matter how great a business idea sounds, the odds are stacked against it. A common trap most people, including athletes, fall into is to invest in businesses that sound cool or have an emotional pull. Examples of these businesses are cafes, fancy restaurants, nightclubs, and other places of entertainment. People think these ventures are profitable because they like the idea of calling themselves owners of successful establishments such as these.

However, all of these businesses are terrible investments because their economics are bad. Why would anyone choose a neighborhood cafe over a Starbucks? Most fancy restaurants close within a year of opening in the United States (*Restaurant Profitability and Failure Rates: What You Need to Know | FSR Magazine*, 2019). As for nightclubs, their appeal is extremely short-lived. Most club owners shut shop and rebrand their venues within a few months.

Successful athletes have many people looking to become freeloaders. These people almost always have these kinds of harebrained business ideas. Establish investments in either of the two categories above (real estate and the stock market) before considering an investment in a private venture.

Technology and apps have become hot thanks to the digital economy. Do not invest in any company you cannot understand. I'll detail the investment criteria you must follow shortly. These apply to all kinds of businesses. If you wish to invest in a business, you need to understand that private businesses are rarely passive. You will need to be involved in them regularly, and they can turn into a full-time job. If this is your aim, then feel free to invest in them. However, please don't assume that they're your only option.

Franchises are the best investment you can make. Not only will you gain the brand power of a successful business, but you'll also receive advice from the business with regards to business best practices. This doesn't mean franchise investments aren't risk-free. It's just that your risk is lower with this option than choosing to start a business of your own. It's not a coincidence that some of the most successful athlete investments have been in successful franchises.

I've already highlighted the example of Shaquille O'Neal and his Five Guys and Krispy Kreme investments. He's also on the board of Papa John's pizza and is a former franchisee. LeBron James successfully invested in Blaze Pizza and helped it become a national chain. This is an example of an investment that is hard to replicate. James invested in a small, local pizza chain that happened to go national. Don't seek to replicate this level of success. I'm not saying this to be pessimistic. It's just that there are easier ways to grow your wealth. Peyton Manning is another example of an athlete who invested in several Papa John's franchises in Denver. He promptly sold them right before the brand was dropped by the NFL and cashed in right at the top.

Franchise business models work pretty much the same way, no matter what the brand is. The franchise (you) needs to pay a certain amount of money to the brand to acquire the rights to use their name at that location. You'll have to pay the rent as well as all expenses related to interior design and inventory (in the case of a fast-food joint, this will be food). From the revenue you earn every month, you'll need to pay royalty fees to the franchise and follow their business operations guidelines.

The advantage is that you can instantly copy and past successful business practices without reinventing the wheel. The brand name alone guarantees some recognition and business. Usually, brands will support their franchisees if the business is slow. It won't be monetary support, but they will boost advertising in your area to drive traffic, along with offering you special promotions. You'll be responsible for staff hiring and salaries. The bottom line profit for most franchisees is between seven to 10% of revenues.

If you own a Krispy Kreme location that sells $1,000 worth of goods every day, this translates to $365,000 worth of sales every year. You can expect to earn $36,500 every year in profits from this location. These numbers are indicative and are for illustration purposes only. You'll need to run the numbers yourself to figure out how much you can earn.

The best way to run these locations is to invest in hiring a business manager. This person will run the day to day operations of your locations and will manage their finances. You'll need to check in with them every week to make sure everything is running smoothly. It's best to hire people from within your network or to hire those who have prior experience. Check with your accountant to find such people. Your accountant will also help you set up a business entity that will safeguard your business interests and ensure your assets are not tied to your business's fortunes. Remember that such investments come after you've got rid of your debt, saved up enough for a freedom fund, and established a real estate stream of income or an investment in the stock market.

Here are a few tips that will help you figure out the investment value of any business.

Do You Understand it?

When someone explains the business to you, do you understand it? Many people invest in businesses they don't understand due to the fear of missing out. They think if they miss this opportunity, they'll never find another investment of the kind. This is incorrect. There are abundant opportunities to grow your money, so don't ever think that you "have" to invest in something.

When examining the business, ask yourself if you can run it yourself. The best business can be run easily. Remember that with investments, your objective is to avoid risk at all costs. If the worst comes to happen and if your manager turns out to be a moron, can you step in and reasonably run the business? If so, invest in it.

Simple Products

What are the products or services that the business offers? Do they have universal appeal? Food is a no-brainer investment. Certain technology apps can also be of this nature; however, make sure you understand them well. Complicated products that require explanation are never good investments. If you can't understand why you'd want to own one, how can you expect someone else to understand them?

Make it a point to examine the investments of other successful people. This is what Shaq did. He's mentioned in the past that he heard Jeff Bezos say that the best investments are the ones that change people's lives and affect them to a great degree. Educate yourself and consume content around investment principles. You'll find yourself learning a lot by emulating the examples of other successful people.

Margins

Margin refers to the amount of money you can earn from the business. Gross margin refers to the difference between a product's cost price and its selling price. A product that costs $10 to make and $20 to sell has a 50% margin. A product that costs $10 to make and $50 to sell has an 80% margin. Net margin refers to whatever is left over after all expenses, including salaries, rental expenses, utilities, and taxes are accounted for. In the case of the $50 product, if you pay $10 in rent, $5 in utilities, $10 as salaries, and $5 as taxes, your total costs are:

Total costs = Product purchase cost + rent utilities + salaries + taxes = 10+10+5+10+5 = $40

Net margin = (Revenues up on sale - total costs)/Revenues = (50-40)/50 = 20%

Gross margins for services are harder to compute. In these cases, examining the net margin is better. Often, when being pitched business ideas, you'll be shown the gross margin figures. Someone might come up to you and say you can buy shoes for $10 in China and sell them for $60 in the United States. You'll earn $50 per shoe, which is 500% of your investment ($50 is your profit, which is 500% of $10). This makes it sound like a wonderful investment. However, this calculation is the wrong way to look at the business. First, ask yourself what the gross margin is. In this case, it's 83%, which is very healthy.

Next, ask yourself what the costs involved in selling the shoe are. You'll need retail space, employees, marketing, electronic systems to track sales, warehouses to store inventory, supply chain systems to ensure inventory is well stocked, and lastly, you'll need to pay taxes. All of these will eat into that gross margin and give you a much lower net margin.

Compare

This step will save you from a world of pain. The net margin of a business is what ultimately goes into your pocket as a business owner. This is what your money is earning. If a business offers you a net margin of just five percent, it makes zero sense for you to invest in it. Why? Because you have your real estate and stock market investments. These are paying you a higher rate of return.

It makes no sense to invest in something that grows your money at a rate below what you can reasonably expect to earn through your other investment methods. You don't need a million different investments to be successful. As Warren Buffett routinely says, you need just two or three very good investments to become wealthy. Focus on quality, not quantity.

Savings Accounts

You might be wondering why I haven't spoken of savings accounts as being legitimate investment options? Well, this has to do with the rate of return they offer. The average savings account offers a paltry sub-one percent return in America right now. This is better than nothing, of course, but it doesn't grow your wealth.

The reason is inflation. Inflation is a hidden cost that all of your investments need to overcome. Currently, the United States experiences inflation of 1.3% per year (*Current US Inflation Rates: 2009-2019*, 2019). This means everything becomes 1.3% more expensive every year. This sounds like a bad thing, but it's quite healthy. An economy that is growing in prosperity will experience healthy inflation levels.

The opposite of inflation is deflation, which indicates that the economy is shrinking and businesses are shutting down on a large scale. An exaggerated version of inflation if hyperinflation, where prices rise uncontrollably. This happens because of economic mismanagement. In the United States, inflation is expected to rise to at least two percent over the next decade. It might even hit four percent.

This means your investments need to grow at this rate at the very least to have an impact. If your savings account pays you less than one percent and if inflation is around 1.3%, you're losing money. This is why you should keep just your freedom cash in your savings account. Put the rest in places where it will grow.

5

RETIREMENT PLANNING

The question isn't at what age I want to retire, it's at what income.

— GEORGE FOREMAN

When you're young, you feel invincible, and retirement seems like a world away. I'm not talking about retiring from the sport you play. I'm talking about actual retirement when your body won't be in the best of shape anymore, and your ability to carry out physical tasks will be compromised. This is the age when injuries will catch up to you, and you'll need additional assistance to live well.

What makes retirement tricky for athletes is that their playing days finish in their early thirties. However, real retirement kicks in only once they turn 60. That's a gap of close to 30 years that's difficult to bridge with just your income from your playing days. If you were lucky enough to earn multimillion-dollar deals in your prime, then you'll have enough to last you a lifetime. Most athletes don't earn anywhere near this kind of money, though.

The First Retirement

Successful retirement planning begins before your playing days are over. The average person can afford to start retirement planning in their forties, but you don't have this luxury. You don't have to think about what life will be like when you're 60, but you need to develop plans for a second career. It's very unlikely that you'll be able to stretch your income from your playing days till retirement. Besides, it's not as if your life is going to end at 60. You can expect to live till you're 80, at the very least.

A second career can involve several things. You could consider coaching or instruction in your sport. Broadcasting is another option that many former athletes use. If you have writing skills, you could consider writing a column for a major magazine and bring insight into your sport. This is what Ross Tucker, a former NFL lineman, did. A journeyman player in the league, injury finally put an end to his career. This led him to chronicle the experience in the noted journalist Peter King's sports column in sports Illustrated. The overwhelming response convinced Tucker to go full time with his writing, and he now hosts his podcast.

If you think you have the chops to be a broadcaster, it's best to start preparing right now. You can easily start your podcast, and bringing guests onto your show won't be an issue thanks to your active connections. Add this to social media exposure on Instagram and Twitter, and you've got yourself a great second career. Who knows, you might even become the next John Madden. Many people forget that Madden was a Super Bowl-winning coach with the Raiders. Before that, he was a pro football player before an injury ended his career.

Another great example of the second and third acts is Steve Spurrier. He's largely known for his time as the University of Florida's football program's head coach. Few remember that he won the Heisman Trophy as a collegiate athlete. He's now a broadcaster on Sirius XM for SEC football games. These are exceptional examples, of course.

Some athletes start successful second careers as business owners.

Former NFL linebacker Brian Orakpo and his former teammate, safety Michael Griffin, are currently the owners of a cupcake shop, which is the last place you'd expect a couple of burly defensive football players to end up. My point with all of these stories is to illustrate that there are always options. It's up to you to sit down and pick the one that appeals to you the most.

There isn't a single path you can take, and this is a good thing. It means you have options. Many athletes decide to return to their alma mater and join the coaching staff. Take the case of Anthony Schlegel, a former linebacker at Ohio State University and the NFL. Following a lackluster professional career, Schlegel joined Ohio State's coaching staff and was struck with an idea for a training machine that players could use.

He quit the staff, got himself an MBA, and patented The Striking Machine. Schlegel is now a successful inventor and runs The Difference USA which markets strength-related products to football programs. All of these stories illustrate the many paths life can take you on once you've left the game. There's no reason for you to be afraid of life after your first career.

If nothing particularly creative strikes you, you can always go back to your alma mater and study for a degree. Universities are very welcoming of former athletes and, in many cases, provide free education or heavily discounted ones. Universities are not the only sources of education. If you happen to be interested in technology and programming, you can study online and join coding boot camps.

Make a list of the things you're passionate about and that you can envision yourself doing 10 or 20 years down the line. Make it a goal to have your new source of active income provide you with at least enough money to cover all of your living expenses. Remember, you'll have set up sources of passive income earlier, so it's not as if you won't have any money coming in.

Begin exploring your options before you retire from your sport. Talk to players who've been through this experience and study examples of former athletes successfully making the transition. If your league has support resources that can help you transition to off-field life, use them. Remember that you don't have to do this all by yourself. Lean of those close to you and seek their help. If your partner or spouse can work at a job, this will bring in additional income.

It's important for the two of you to work as a team and figure out what you want your off-field life to look like. If you're faced with the prospect of living in conditions that are below what you've grown accustomed to, then start planning for it right now. Are you okay with this transition, or do you want to maintain the same standard of living? Not everyone is as lucky as Tony Romo is and can earn more as a broadcaster than they did as a player.

Remember that a decrease in living standards doesn't mean you'll be giving up luxuries forever. You'll need those luxuries when you retire due to old age—plan for those years right now by utilizing all of the investment options available to you.

Retirement Accounts

There are two kinds of retirement accounts you can open. The first is an Individual Retirement Account or IRA. There are two types of IRAs, called the traditional IRA and the Roth IRA. The second type of retirement account is a 401(k), which you were briefly introduced to previously. Let's deal with IRAs first.

IRAs are called tax-deferred accounts. The way they work is simple. All of the money you invest in an IRA is non-taxable until you reach 59 ½. You can withdraw your money at this age and will have to pay taxes on your withdrawal at ordinary income tax rates. I'll explain the deal with taxes in the next chapter. Ordinary income tax rates are the same as the taxes you pay on your current earnings.

If you withdraw your money before the age of 59 ½, you will pay a penalty of 10% of your withdrawal amount, and you'll pay taxes on the withdrawal. Once you reach the age of 70, you'll be forced to withdraw money from your IRA. There are minimum amounts of money you'll have to withdraw every year after this age.

The benefits of an IRA lie mostly in their ability to defer taxes. If you buy a stock for $10 and sell it for $20, you don't need to pay taxes on it if you've done this in an IRA account. A regular broker will help you open an IRA without any issues, so it's not as if you'll have to deal

Athlete Finance

with a mountain of paperwork. The biggest benefit of a traditional IRA is that you'll be contributing pre-tax dollars to this account. For example, you could allocate $2,000 of your pre-tax income to your IRA account and invest this into the market. You'll, therefore, not pay income tax on this amount before investing it.

Let's look at the potential gains via an example. Let's say you receive $2,000 as income. You'll have to pay taxes on this. Let's say you pay 10% as taxes. This reduces your income available to $1,800. You invest this money into stocks and let's say, after a year, you earn a gain of 10%. You decide to sell your investment, at which point you'll need to pay taxes. For simplicity's sake, let's say this tax rate is also 10%. You're now left with:

Initial investment = $1,800
Gain = 10% of $1,800 = $180
New balance before taxes = initial investment + gain = $1,980
Tax rate = 10%
Tax amount = 10% of gains = 180*.1 = $18
New balance after taxes = Balance before taxes - tax amount = 1980 - 18 = $1,962

Let's assume you invest this new amount into another opportunity that nets you 10% once again. You'll again pay 10% in taxes. Your new balance is now:

Initial investment = $1,962
Gain = 10% of $1,800 = $196.2
New balance before taxes = initial investment + gain = $2,158.2
Tax rate = 10%
Tax amount = 10% of gains = 180*.1 = $19.62
New balance after taxes = Balance before taxes - tax amount = 2,158.2 - 19.62 = $2,138.58

You're still making money, but as you can see, you received $2,000 before taxes initially, and in two years, you've grown this to $2,138.58. How would this picture change if you had contributed $2,000 into an IRA? Your contribution is non-taxable, so that you would have deposited the full $2,000 into the account.

After the first year, this would have grown to $2,200. There are no taxes to be paid if you sell this investment. You would have invested this entire amount into the second investment and gained 10% on that to leave you with $2,420 at the end of the second year. This is compared to $2,139 in the case of taxable income. That's a difference of 12% over just two years. Let's say this picture remains the same till you reach the age of 69 ½. You'll pay taxes on the withdrawal. Once again, let's assume this is 10%. Your overall gain has been (2,420-2,000) $420. 10% of this is $42. Your final amount after taxes is $2,378.

This is 11% greater than the case where you invested taxable income. Using an IRA has made you 11% more money, and this is just over two years. Over the course of 20 or 25 years, you can expect far greater gains. IRA contributions are currently capped at $6,000 per year, which doesn't sound like much (Retirement Topics - IRA Contribution Limits | Internal Revenue Service, 2019). However, given how they boost your gains, it makes sense to contribute this amount in full.

Roth IRAs work a bit differently than traditional IRAs. For starters, you cannot contribute pre-tax dollars into a Roth. Your post-tax income can be contributed and will not attract any taxes until withdrawal at the age of 59 ½ and above. Roth contribution limits are the same as traditional IRAs. However, they depend on your filing type and income (Retirement Topics - IRA Contribution Limits | Internal Revenue Service, 2019). You should check with your accountant or with the IRS to figure out the latest information since this changes every year.

The advantage of a Roth IRA is that you don't need to pay taxes on your earnings for certain types of withdrawals. If you're withdrawing your money after you're 59 ½ years old, and if you have a permanent disability, or if your beneficiary is withdrawing the money after your death, or if you're withdrawing a sum of $100,000 to build your first home, these withdrawals are tax-free.

Note that only your earnings are tax-free. Your contributions are not taxed, unlike the case with a traditional IRA. For example, let's say you invested $6,000 into an IRA and $6,000 into a Roth IRA. Let's assume both of these investments grew to $6,600, at which point you've decided to withdraw them once you reach the age of 60.

With the traditional IRA, the tax authorities will add the $6,600 to your overall income and ask you to pay taxes according to the relevant tax bracket you fit into. If you earned $55,000 during the year, your taxable income would be (55,000+6,000) $61,000. This is not the case with the Roth IRA. If you earned $55,000 during the year, your taxable income would be this amount plus whatever gains your investment experienced.

Thus, you'll pay taxes on (55,000+600) $55,600. This results in a lower tax bill. The reason for this is your contributions to a Roth IRA have already been taxed before they were deposited. In contrast, the ones to your traditional IRA weren't. Remember how you diverted them before you received any money? Speak to a financial advisor to determine which choice is better for you. A lot depends on your financial situation, so it's best to seek professional help.

Let's leave the world of IRAs behind for now and examine the 401(k). As you've already learned, these retirement accounts provide you the benefit of employer matching. Take full advantage of this since this is free money. Happily, 401(k) contribution limits are much higher than IRAs. The annual limit is $19,500.

401(k)s can also be traditional or Roth, depending on the type of contributions you're making. Given the advantages of employer matching, making pre-tax contributions is the best move forward. Maximize these contributions and employer matching, and you'll earn a ton of money over time. It's not very common these days, but some leagues offer managed 401(k) plans. The idea is that your league contracts an investment firm to manage the assets in the 401(k).

You can opt for these but make sure you have your passive investments setup as described before. If you end up having more than one employer, then you can have two 401(k) plans but your overall contribution per year needs to be under the limit. If you feel confused by these options, consult a financial advisor, and ask them for help.

Your Second Retirement

At some point in time, you're going to have to figure out what kind of life you want after you turn 60. You can continue to work after that age, but physically, you're going to face limitations. Some of your old injuries will catch up, and you might need physical assistance. Most people usually start planning for this phase of life in their forties, and it will most likely be the same for you as well.

Take some time and make a list of all the things you want in your life at that age. Where will you live? What will you do during the day, and how will you occupy yourself? If you plan on traveling, then you need to account for these costs as well. Involve your partner and discuss everything with them in detail.

By that age, you'll have paid off your properties and will own them fully. You will have enough income coming in passively to give you steady cash flow. Cash flow is extremely important when you retire because it increases your net worth or paper money doesn't serve you anymore. What is the use of you worth a billion on paper if you don't have the cash to pay your medical bills? Besides, you can only leave your heirs so much money. There's no point continuing to accumulate large gains on paper unless you're truly interested in doing so.

You can shift your portfolio towards income-generating strategies. Dividend investing is one way of doing this. Instead of reinvesting your dividends, you could elect to receive them as cash. You can invest in bond ETFs that will pay you a certain amount of money every year. Perhaps the best retirement solution is an annuity.

Annuities are offered by insurance companies and are a great way to receive a pension in retirement. There are different types of annuities, but all of them work on the same basic premise. They work because you pay the insurance company a certain sum of money and tell them when you wish to start receiving monthly payments and how much you want those payments to be. Depending on these conditions, you'll have to invest a certain amount of cash.

The longer you choose to delay payments, and the older you are, the higher your monthly payments will be. You can choose different kinds of payout structures as well. You can choose to have them pay you till the end of your lifetime, beyond the end of your life to your heirs or spouse until the money you invested runs out, the payout for a minimum number of years (usually 10) and then refund you the remaining amount, or pay you till the end of your life and then refund you the remaining amount.

As you can see, there are several combinations, so it's best to talk to a financial advisor and understand your options. Start preparing in your forties, so that you'll have a steady stream of cash when you're older. Annuities don't provide you with the highest return rates on your money, but they provide you steady cash flow. As you reach the end of your life, growing money isn't much of a concern as receiving cash to live is.

If everything has gone according to plan, you'll have a decent number of assets to look after in your old age. As you take stock of how things are likely to pan out when you're 40, you need to think about drafting a will and planning these assets' disposal. By disposal, I don't mean selling them. Instead, think about how you'd like to deal with them. You can pass them onto your heirs, or you could sell it and invest that money elsewhere.

If you have the cash, you should also consider setting up a trust fund for your children or heirs. The way it works is much like an annuity. You invest a sum of money, and your heirs get paid a fixed amount of cash every month after reaching a certain age. How much you want them to be paid every month depends on you. You could go the Warren Buffett way and leave them with close to nothing, or you could go the Bill Gates way and leave them with just enough not to be poor but not so much that they won't need to work for a living.

Your health will be of major concern as you grow old, so you should take the time to schedule regular doctor's visits and prepare to address any injuries that will worsen. Knees and ankles are usually what goes first, especially if you've played a contact sport. Consider whether you'll need a mobility scooter once you're older and plan on investing in one right now. This could be as simple as checking which insurers provide this facility and how much it will cost.

You might also need to look at your living arrangements and make changes to your home. If need be, you might have to move to a new home to facilitate your new lifestyle. It will be tough to think of everything this much in advance but remember to view everything through the prism of risk. Work to mitigate risk as much as possible, and you're less likely to deal with nasty surprises.

Like with investing, proper retirement planning is a question of educating yourself. Speak to counselors and use the help of organizations to advise you on the best move for your future. Just like with all of your endeavors on the field, prepare as much as possible in advance, and you'll be well set to handle retirement and all of its challenges. The most important thing is for you to get serious about it.

Unlike regular people, you have two retirements to deal with. It can be hard to say goodbye to the game you've played since you were a kid but don't overstay your welcome and put your body at greater risk than strictly needed. The injuries you sustain today will present their bill when you're older. Speak to older players in your sport to gain perspective on how you can take better care of yourself.

Your first retirement will give you a good perspective on your second. When you retire from your playing days, you'll be tempted to think of yourself as old, but in terms of regular life, you're just entering your prime. The average retirement age of an athlete is around 31 years old. In the real world, a 31-year-old is just getting started on the prime of their lives. Never forget this. You're not old. You've just achieved a lot at a very young age.

You're now all set to achieve even more, which will prepare you to live peacefully and well during your old age. Prepare all the way, and you'll be just fine.

6

TAXES

Our new Constitution is now established, everything seems to promise it will be durable; but, in this world, nothing is certain except death and taxes.

— BENJAMIN FRANKLIN

Contrary to what you might be expecting, this chapter isn't going to be too long. I understand that taxes can be dry and boring, and they often consume numerous volumes. Well, none of that is going to happen here. As far as taxes go, they're quite simple to deal with as long as you follow the rules and don't get too adventurous.

There are two levels of taxes you'll have to deal with. The first is personal tax, and the second is business tax. Let's look at personal taxes first.

Personal Income Taxes

There are two types of personal income tax you will pay. The first is ordinary income tax, and the second is capital gains taxes. Here's where it can get confusing. Capital gains taxes, which you pay on investment gains, are of two types, short-term and long-term. If you held your investment for less than a year before selling it, this is a short term investment. Short term capital gains taxes are equal to ordinary income taxes. Long term capital gains taxes, applicable on investments you help for more than a year before selling, are lower than ordinary income taxes and depend on your regular income.

Ordinary income tax rates are determined based on the tax bracket you fall into and how you're filing your taxes. You can file taxes as an individual, jointly with your spouse, separately with your spouse (it makes no sense in English, but the tax code has its own weird rules) and as a head of a household. The brackets have minimum and maximum incomes and a tax rate that goes along with them. For example, if you file as a single person, all income you earn up to $9,875 will be taxed at 10%.

For the latest income tax brackets, you can visit https://www.nerdwallet.com/article/taxes/federal-income-tax-brackets. This link will provide you with the relevant tables to detail your tax rate according to your filing status. Something to note about these tax brackets is that they're progressive. Let's say you earn $50,000 per year. The first $9,875 is taxed at 10%, the next $40,125 is taxed at 12%, and the remaining amount is taxed at 22%.

The income you earn in the form of cash flow will be taxed at ordinary income tax rates. For example, the rental cash flow that you earn will be taxed as ordinary income. Suppose you draw a salary for yourself from your business or pay yourself a dividend. In that case, it is taxed as ordinary income. There are ways to lower your tax bill using a business; I'll discuss business taxation shortly.

Capital gains occur when you sell an asset for a higher price than what you bought it for. If you buy a stock for $10 and sell it for $20 a year later, you'll pay long-term capital gains taxes on the profit you earned from the sale. Long term capital gains tax rates are significantly lower than ordinary income tax rates. This is why it makes sense to hang onto your investments for at least one year. Not only does this give your investment more time to grow, but it also reduces your tax bill massively. Of course, the ideal timeline is greater than ten years since it takes this long for any asset to appreciate.

Long term capital gains tax rates can be found at this link: https://www.investopedia.com/articles/personal-finance/101515/comparing-longterm-vs-short term-capital-gain-tax-rates.asp. Like ordinary income taxes, the tax you pay depends on your filing status, as well as your current marginal income tax bracket. The highest tax rate you'll pay is 20%. This is in comparison to a maximum rate of 37% when it comes to ordinary income taxes.

You can reduce your tax bill in several ways. This is done by claiming deductions. Let's look at how this works.

Deductions

Deductions are exactly what their name suggests they are. They're items you can use to reduce your tax bill. There are two broad categories of deductions you can apply. The first is a standard deduction. Think of this as a discount that the government gives every taxpayer, free of charge. The standard deduction amount varies depending on your filing status. For 2020, here are the deduction amounts (Kagan, 2020):

- $12,200 for single taxpayers
- $12,200 for married taxpayers filing separately
- $18,350 for heads of households
- $24,400 for married taxpayers filing jointly
- $24,400 for qualifying widow(er)s

If you're single and are earning $80,000 per year, a $12,200 deduction in your taxes works out to a reduction of 15%, which is significant. Let's say you contribute the maximum amount of $19,000 into your 401(k) before taxes. This reduces your taxable income to (80,000-19,000) $61,000. Apply the standard deduction of $12,200 to this, and your taxable income is now (61,000-12,200) $48,800. Not bad at all! You'll be paying taxes on just a little more than half of your pre-tax income. Of course, you'll have to pay taxes on your 401(k) on withdrawal down the road, but you can grow that money for many years before paying taxes.

The standard deduction is chosen by most people when filing taxes because the other option, itemized deductions, doesn't always make sense. There are certain items that the IRS allows you to deduct from your income when filing taxes. The catch is that you can either itemize your deductions or claim the standard deduction. You can't claim both. For most people, their itemized deductions (of which you need to have records) don't add up to a greater amount than the standard deduction.

If you own property, this is unlikely to be the case. Here's why real estate is such a great investment. You can deduct practically everything that goes into maintaining your property, including your mortgage interest payment. Recall that you learned earlier that the monthly mortgage payment contains a principal portion and an interest portion. You can deduct that interest paid from your taxes. Therefore, your real expense is just the principal you pay your lender every month.

You can also deduct maintenance expenses, property taxes, mortgage insurance if you have any policies and other miscellaneous items. If you paid any local taxes (property taxes, for example), you could deduct these as well. There is a limit to the amount of local taxes you can deduct. You (or your accountant) will need to evaluate whether these individual deductions add up to a greater sum than the standard deduction. If it does, be prepared for the IRS to ask you for receipts and proof. This is why maintaining good records is essential—document everything.

Compared to real estate, stock market investments do not offer the potential for deductions. Dividends will be taxed as ordinary income. Capital gains will be treated accordingly, depending on how long you held onto the investment. Your broker will provide you with a Form 1099-DIV that will list how your dividends and capital gains should be treated. Your accountant will use this form to prepare your taxes.

Dividend taxation is complex, but I'm not diving into it for many reasons. For starters, it's irrelevant to you. You cannot control how your dividends will be treated. Secondly, your broker will identify how they ought to be treated on the 1099-DIV, so unless you have an academic interest in how they're treated, diving into dividend taxation makes no sense. If you are interested in understanding qualified versus non-qualified dividends, I suggest reading Investopedia or speaking to an accountant.

That's all there is to know about personal taxes. You contribute as much as you can pre-tax into your retirement accounts, claim either the standard deduction or an itemized list (with proof), and pay your taxes according to which ever tax bracket you land in.

Business Taxes

Business taxes are a bit more complex, but they can save you money. This is especially true if you have large business interests. Let's say you own more than ten properties and are collecting rent on them, or if you own an apartment block, it makes sense to own these investments through a company. The taxes you pay depends on your company's structure. Here are the three most common structures utilized by investors.

Limited Liability Company

The LLC is the most used business structure. The idea behind this corporate structure is that any liability claims that result from business malpractice are restricted to the assets that the business owns and don't extend to the owner's assets. Reads like a bunch of legalese, doesn't it? Well, here's an example to show you how it works. Let's say you own a restaurant, and some knucklehead decides to swallow a straw on purpose. They choke from it and almost die.

They sue you in court, claiming that you didn't warn them that swallowing the straw would be dangerous. The judge decides this is a reasonable argument and orders you to pay damages to the extent of $1 million for causing distress. Here's where the LLC protects you. If your business has assets worth $500,000, you don't need to pay them a dime more than this amount. If you don't have an LLC, the judge could order you to sell your assets, such as a rental property not connected to your restaurant or your investments in the stock market, to compensate the moron suing you.

I'm exaggerating the type of suit you could face in court. However, this sort of thing is extremely common in America and Canada. This is why every property you buy has homeowner's insurance. If someone trips on the sidewalk in front of your home and injures themselves, they might be able to sue you in court for damages. An LLC is a layer of protection and prevents people from targeting their assets. If you're rich enough, holding your prized assets in an offshore LLC can protect them from divorce settlements as well.

The great thing about an LLC is that its tax structure is simple. All income is treated as "passing through." In taxman-speak, this means the LLC itself doesn't earn anything. It simply receives all the money and passes them onto you. If you own an LLC, you'll need to file accounting statements with the IRS and then pay taxes on that income as a part of your income tax filing in April.

The downside of an LLC is that it makes business growth difficult. Let's say you own a restaurant through an LLC and decide that instead of paying yourself a salary, it would be better to reinvest those profits back into the business to earn more money down the road. With an LLC, you can't simply reinvest profits. You'll need to pay taxes on those profits and reinvest whatever is leftover. This makes business growth tough. This is why many business people prefer the corporation.

Corporations

Corporations are also referred to as C-Corps. They're treated as separate entities and aren't pass-through as LLCs are. They're living, breathing things, and need to be treated as such. You'll need to appoint a Board of Directors and elect officers. The board will need to meet at least once a year, and notes of that meeting need to be maintained. The corporation will file its taxes and profit and loss statements.

The IRS also stipulates that corporations need to pay taxes preemptively. This means that your accountant will need to project how much profit you can expect to earn and pay a certain amount of tax to the IRS every month. This amount paid is adjusted against your actual profit or loss at the end of the year, and the money is refunded, or you'll pay the balance. It takes a lot of time and effort to run a corporation.

The advantage is that since it's a separate entity, it can reinvest its profits as operating expenditures and not pay taxes on this. Your accountant, if they're honest, will warn you not to reinvest everything as operating expenses. Instead, they'll push you to classify the majority of expenses as capital expenditures or capex. Capex is the money you spend creating an asset for the business. Capex cannot be fully deducted; only a portion of it can be applied against income. The reality is that lines can blur between capex and operating expenses.

Let's say you invest in better chairs for your restaurants. Is this an operating or capital expense? Chairs can be considered inventory to deduct it from income like you would deduct the cost of buying food. However, chairs make your restaurant more attractive to customers and enhance your asset to be capex. Accountants need to make subjective judgments. To avoid getting into trouble, take the time to get to know the person's ethics, preparing your books. Stick to people who come recommended by others and have a stellar reputation.

You can pay yourself a salary every month from the company, whether it makes money or not. You don't want to pay yourself if the company isn't earning anything. This salary will be treated as ordinary income. The business will file its taxes, and you'll pay the amount due from its bank account.

S Corps

S corps are a combination of LLCs and C Corps. The problem with C Corps is that you'll pay taxes twice. The business pays taxes on its earnings, and you pay taxes on the salary you draw or dividends you pay yourself. The S Corp affords you the benefits of a corporation but has the pass-through nature of an LLC.

The money you pay yourself as salary (not dividends) can be deducted as business expenses, and you'll pay a reduced amount of taxes. Some clever people look at this as a license to deduct their entire profit as salary and find that the IRS comes down on them like a pack of hounds. S Corps are heavily scrutinized, and you need to make sure your accountant is a person of high ethics if you decide to go down this route. If any scandal ensues, you're the one who'll be in the spotlight, not them.

Using Legal Entities

The LLC is the most commonly used entity when it comes to athlete investments. They're easy to incorporate, and their taxes are simple. The key is to create a separate bank account for the LLC to separate your personal assets from your LLCs assets. You can invest in ventures using your LLCs money and will be protected from any liability claims. A good accountant will help you understand how you can protect yourself even more by managing your LLCs assets intelligently.

For example, you shouldn't place all your investment assets in an LLC. If you do get sued, you'll lose everything. It makes sense to set up different entities to hold different assets. Keep in mind that when it comes to real estate, banks do not prefer to lend to LLCs. They prefer lending to individuals. Most people apply for mortgages in their names and then transfer the property to their LLC. You'll need to take care of some legal formalities, so speak to your accountant about doing this.

If you've been following, your accountant is a crucial part of your tax and business picture. Ask for references and only choose those professionals who have a high reputation. If you're using a personal financial advisor, ask them for references. Ask your teammates or other people who own businesses for references to good accountants.

A common question is, should you consult an attorney or an accountant? When it comes to business matters, consulting an accountant makes more sense. This doesn't mean an attorney can't help you. Many athletes conduct their business through an attorney who manages all of their interests. Suppose you employ an attorney to handle the legalities of your businesses. In that case, you're outsourcing the choice of accountant and business ventures to them. If you can afford the services of one, it makes sense to do this. If you prefer a more hands-on approach, choosing to work directly with an accountant makes sense.

When it comes to tax affairs and company matters, the lines can blur between both professionals, so choosing either one makes sense. Just make sure they're highly reputable and have a high standard of ethics. Do not choose your close friends to represent you just because you know them well.

7

LEGAL HELP, ATHLETE IMAGE ENTITIES, AND FINANCIAL ADVISORS

Laws are like cobwebs, which may catch small flies, but let wasps and hornets break through.

— JONATHAN SWIFT

As an athlete, your image is your most treasured asset. In the past, bodies such as the NCAA used student-athlete images to earn billions of dollars. However, they treated the athletes themselves as indentured workers. This is changing, and it opens many athletes to the existence of athlete image entities. These entities are companies, much like the ones you learned about in the previous chapter, with the difference that their assets are intellectual, not physical.

Famous athletes utilize this arrangement all the time. Let's say Nike wishes to use LeBron James' image for their campaigns. They pay James' company a sponsorship fee and pay him royalties for the right to use his image. The company that holds the rights to license James' image is separate from the one that collects his sponsorship payments, to protect his assets from being exposed to a liability suit.

The way it works is that your image and everything connected to it, such as your social media accounts and any other intangible thing contributing to your image, is treated as intellectual property (IP). The IP is transferred to a firm. This might be hard to visualize, but it's all paperwork. You're the company owner, and the IP is just a bunch of paperwork that defines what the IP is.

Suppose anyone wants to use your image or its likeness, along with any signature phrases or anything else associated with you. In that case, they'll have to pay you license fees. This is why athletes are so conscious of their image in public. Famous athletes earn much money by licensing their images. If they speak out in public about controversial issues, they lose much money from the companies paying them licensing fees. Celebrities such as actors and reality TV stars use this tactic as well.

Often, phrases can be trademarked as well. This doesn't always work out since the trademarking language is tricky. A good example of this occurred in the previous decade when reality TV star Paris Hilton tried to trademark her signature phrase, "That's hot." A judge ruled that this amounted to trademarking the English language. However, her request was granted, and the use of this phrase in certain situations and on certain products such as clothing, electronic devices, and alcohol is trademarked (Protecting the Money Maker: 5 Celebrity Trademarks, 2020)

There have been athletes who have tried to generate additional cash through their name changing stuns. The former NFL wide receiver Chad Johnson changed his last name to "Ochocinco" and trademarked a logo around the name. Joel Embiid, the NBA player, trademarked items that refer to "The Process," Shaquille O'Neal has trademarked the phrase "Shaq Attack," Jeremy Lin "Linsanity," and so on. All of these trademarks are owned by image entities and constitute the IP that these companies own.

In the previous chapter, I addressed whether you need to approach a lawyer or an accountant to form companies. In the case of athlete image entities, a lawyer is the one you want to approach since trademarking and IP creation falls under the legal umbrella. It's helpful to set up an initial consultation with a reputed law firm to determine whether setting up such an entity makes sense for you.

Legal Help

If your profile is big enough to warrant it, hiring a law firm to handle your affairs is a good move. How do you know if your profile is high enough? For starters, do you have local firms chasing you to sign sponsorships? If yes, then you have a high profile. Many people target athletes and their money. The minute your image is out in public, you need to start protecting yourself.

A law firm can provide you with a wide range of assistance. Let's look at some of the services these firms offer.

Real Estate Services

A critical part of your real estate investments are the leases you'll sign. The lease is a legal agreement that governs your relationship with your tenants. At some point, you're going to have to deal with a painful tenant who creates problems for you. You'll need to follow the procedures as laid out by the law and ensure you don't violate your tenant's rights in the process. Doing so could result in even more delays and a cash flow hole for you.

A good law firm will walk you through your lease's specifics and help you understand how you can structure it to protect yourself as an owner or as a tenant. Athletes need to lease temporary places all the time, thanks to spring training and offseason camps. Some of these leases can be tricky, so it's best to use expert help.

Financing and the mortgage application process are also tricky situations to navigate. You need expert legal help to find your way through it. It especially makes sense the first few times since you're unlikely to be familiar with how the process works.

Litigation

As an athlete with a profile, you are a target. People will sue you for stupid reasons to drag your name through the mud in the hopes that you'd rather settle than proceed to court and have embarrassing claims come to light. It isn't just issued that surrounds your playing career but other issues such as tenants suing you for weird reasons, financial advisors potentially entangling you in bad situations, and so on.

Having a good law firm by your side acts as an insurance policy. The people who serially sue famous people are aware of the law firms' reputations connected to their targets. Hire a strong law firm, and these freeloaders usually back away from you.

Corporate Services

Suppose you're going to be investing in and protecting your assets. In that case, you will need to form entities that do so effectively. Not only will you need to set up the right kinds of entities, but you'll also need to distribute your assets optimally between all of them. The services of a reputed law firm will help you figure out the maze of legalities you'll need to take care of.

You'll also need to handle legal matters related to the companies you set up, such as signing corporate charter papers and filing minutes of meetings. You can do all of this by yourself, but this will likely cut into your training time. It's best to outsource this to competent lawyers who can help you with everything.

Family Law

Athletes get divorced all the time, and other prickly family issues often arise when money enters the picture. Issues such as child custody, support, and divorce are sensitive issues. You don't want any of this spilling into the public eye, thereby damaging your image. A good law firm will help you navigate these muddy waters easily.

Taxes and Estate Planning

As I mentioned in an earlier chapter, you need to start planning for retirement during your playing days. You can't kick the can down the road and hope to pick the issue up later. A good lawyer will help you set up trusts, and other vehicles that can safeguard your wealth and will ensure your assets are disposed of in the manner you desire.

Take your time to hire a good lawyer. The right lawyer or law firm will be your greatest asset since they'll make several things simple for you. Once again, don't hire the person who's close to you just because of their proximity. Evaluate whether they're truly qualified to run your assets and advise you.

Evaluating Financial Advisors

Professional athletes are often bombarded with recommendations for financial advisors. Using an advisor is a good move if your finances intimidate you or unsure how a particular investment opportunity works. It would help if you were wary of financial advisors. This isn't because they don't know what they're talking about or because they're incompetent.

They tend to lack personal experience with large sums of money and are not good business people. For example, a financial advisor would have never signed off on an investment such as LeBron James' Blaze Pizza investment. They would have instead recommended he place that money in bonds or stocks.

The issue isn't necessarily with the advisors themselves. There's also a problem in how society views their services. We expect them to know everything about money and expect them to evaluate every business opportunity with aplomb. If they truly had this ability, they'd be billionaires themselves and wouldn't be dispensing financial advice. The solution is to utilize its services effectively.

You can do this by asking them how an investment product works and telling them to explain its pros and cons in great detail. Do not be swayed by the way they look at risk. Every individual has their definition of risk, and their definition is not necessarily yours. The risk ladder that I presented previously in the chapter on investments, which went from real estate to the stock market to private businesses, is enough to help you determine how risky a business opportunity might be.

Once they've described the pros and cons to you, check whether you understand how the opportunity works. If you don't understand it, move on and wait for something else to come knocking. Remember that you won't miss out on huge opportunities if you forego a few. If you choose to stay away from opportunities you don't understand, you're not missing out on anything. Would you expect an engineer to perform the duties of a surgeon? Is the engineer preceding a golden opportunity if they elect not to perform surgery on someone? Of course not.

Here is an easy process that will help you figure out whether an advisor is worth your time.

Preliminary Work

Take some time to figure out your financial goals. It could be as simple as "I want a million dollars in the bank," or it could be more sophisticated as "I want to set up a trust fund for my kids and an annuity for my partner and I in 25 years." Write all of these down. Also, write down the things you understand about finance and investment and the things you don't.

Whether you know it or not, you have financial skills. Skills such as budgeting and getting rid of debt are all about habits. As long as you have the strength to follow the habits that will help you stay on track, they're easy to do. Investment skills require work. This is why I suggested a very simple investment template for you. Stay away from investing in individual companies because you need a host of other skills to do this successfully.

Lastly, examine your expectations. Markets don't always go up. It's easy to make money in rising markets. Markets that decline are what separate the wheat from the chaff. You cannot expect your investments to increase in value constantly. There will be times when you'll make a sound investment only to see your investment has declined in value. Remember that you aim to remain invested for more than 15 years at the very least. Fix these correct expectations in your head and drive the incorrect ones away. Check to see if you're trying to get rich(er) quick. Those schemes always lead to losses.

Questions to Ask an Advisor

The first question to ask is whether they get paid commissions based on the products they recommend. Every advisor gets paid commissions for recommending certain mutual funds or investment products. Honest advisors let their clients know and discuss all the options on the table. Dishonest ones might not disclose commissions or might disclose it but not provide you with any other alternatives.

Ask them what their fee structure is and what your all-in costs are. Most advisors charge a percentage of the assets they manage. This is usually one percent. An important question to ask them is what kind of tax bill you will face by investing with them. Some advisors might trade over the short term frequently. While this will earn you a profit (or it might not), you'll pay far higher taxes. Stick to advisors who espouse a long term view of 15 years or more.

Check to see if they've hired a custodian for your money. A custodian is a brokerage firm that holds your funds in an account under your name. Some financial advisors act as their custodians and hold clients' money in their accounts. These kinds of advisors are almost always charlatans, so don't trust them. A financial advisor is not a hedge fund manager. They should not be holding your money for you.

Speaking of hedge fund managers, you need to recognize what realistic market returns are. Any business that returns 15% or more on the amount of money invested is exceptional. There are very few businesses in the world that will bring you this kind of return. If you invest in a restaurant franchise, you can expect around 7-10% as annual returns. I've already listed the average return you can expect with a stock market investment.

Real estate returns are very high, but this is because you'll be borrowing most of the money you need to buy a property. If you buy a property for cash, you can reasonably expect between 7-10% returns every year from the rental income. I'm detailing these numbers because you might have someone slide up to you and propose a venture that returns 20% per month. These are ridiculous numbers, and it's impossible to generate such returns. If these returns were true, Jeff Bezos is probably better off selling his Amazon shares and investing in this venture.

Ask your advisor what they think about certain businesses to get a feel for their risk tolerance. The objective isn't to see whether they give you a right or wrong answer. Instead, it's to see how conservative they are. This might sound odd, but you want to go with an advisor who is more conservative than you. This will prevent you from overextending yourself, and you'll always have a voice that counsels caution. This is very important when evaluating an investment since it can be easy to get caught up in your narrative and ignore counter-evidence.

If you are entrusting all of your money to the advisor, notice how they talk about generating investment returns. If they promise to double your money in a year or some such nonsense, run away from them. It doesn't matter if they've done this with someone else; you won't be missing out on anything by investing with such a person. If they promote some secret sauce or present themselves as being a genius, run away. Choose a person who is normal and is downright boring. This person will never leave you sleepless at night, worrying about the state of your money.

Ask them what their benchmarks are. A benchmark is a scale you can compare their performance to. Most advisors will choose the S&P 500. Underperformance in good years isn't always bad as long as they consistently outperform in bad years. Ask them for their track record and question them about it. Ask them which strategies they pursue, what asset allocation they followed, and why they underperformed. Remember, underperformance or losing money in a year or even two years isn't a bad thing. You want to see how honest they are about their mistakes and the lessons they've learned.

Trust your instincts and see whether you like them as a person. More often than not, this will alert you to situations that are too good to be true.

EPILOGUE

Despite what your advisors and those around you might say, always remember that it's your money. You're the one in charge, and you have the final say-so when it comes to making investment choices. You're also in full control of your budget and debt levels. Remember the lessons about creating an asset versus a liability and aim to create as many assets as possible. Minimize your liabilities and stay away from stupid decisions. This alone will ensure you'll take the right steps when it comes to your finances.

Throughout this book, my mission has been to empower you to make your own decisions. If you feel less than capable, seek help. I've given you helpful pointers on how you can evaluate the quality of such help as well. You don't necessarily need to hire a financial advisor to be successful with your investments. However, it would help if you made the right decisions. If you feel as if you can't do this, seek help. If you can, then view everything from the standpoint of risk.

Risk evaluation comes down to this: If the investment doesn't work out, how much of a hole will you be in? What is the likelihood of the investment not working out? For example, if a stock market index investment doesn't work out, you'll likely be in a big hole since you'll be investing much money into it. However, the likelihood of it not working out, in the long run, is slim. Hence, you can justify placing much money into it.

A private business has a higher chance of going belly up than the entire stock market. Therefore, invest a small amount of money into it and take more time understanding everything about it. Plan your taxes and other legalities well, and always remember to plan for your retirement, both of them. I wish you all the prosperity in the world.

THE SCIENCE OF ATHLETIC PERFORMANCE

FROM ANATOMY AND PHYSIOLOGY TO GENETICS, TRAINING, NUTRITION, PEDS, PSYCHOLOGY, RECOVERY AND INJURY PREVENTION, TECHNOLOGY, AND ENVIRONMENTAL FACTORS

INTRODUCTION

The science of athletic performance is a **complex** and **multifaceted** field that encompasses various disciplines, including anatomy and physiology, training, nutrition, psychology, and technology. Understanding the science behind the athletic performance is crucial for athletes who want to reach their full potential and achieve their goals.

This book will explore the key factors contributing to athletic performance and how we can optimize them. We will cover a wide range of topics, including the anatomy and physiology of athletic performance, genetics, training principles, nutrition, performance enhancing substances, psychological factors, recovery and injury prevention, the role of technology, and environmental factors.

Unleashing Your Inner Athlete

A combination of physical, mental, and technical factors determines athletic performance. Physical factors include strength, power, endurance, and flexibility, which are influenced by genetics, training, and nutrition. Mental factors such as motivation, confidence, focus, and stress management can significantly impact athletic performance. Finally, technical factors such as technique and tactics can also play a

Introduction

crucial role in athletic performance, particularly in sports that require specific skills or strategies.

By understanding the science behind athletic performance, athletes and coaches can develop effective training programs, nutrition plans, and mental skills training tailored to the individual's specific needs and goals. This can help athletes optimize their physical and mental performance, reduce the risk of injury, and ultimately achieve their goals.

Scope of the Book

This book is designed to provide a comprehensive overview of the key factors that contribute to athletic performance and how we can optimize them. We will delve into the anatomy and physiology of athletic performance, including the musculoskeletal system, the cardiovascular and respiratory systems, and the role of energy production and utilization. We will also explore training principles, including periodization, strength training, and skill development.

In addition to the physical aspects of athletic performance, we will also examine the psychological factors that can impact an athlete's performance, such as motivation, confidence, focus, and stress management. We will also discuss the importance of recovery and injury prevention in maintaining optimal performance. Finally, we will explore the role of technology in athletic performance, including wearable technology and data analysis to track and improve performance.

This introduction outlines the importance of understanding the science behind athletic performance and the book's scope. In the coming chapters, we will delve deeper into each of these topics, drawing upon the latest research and best practices to provide a comprehensive and practical guide to optimizing athletic performance. So, whether you are an athlete looking to improve your performance or a coach seeking to help your athletes reach their full potential, this book is designed to provide you with the knowledge and tools you need to succeed.

1
ANATOMY AND PHYSIOLOGY OF ATHLETIC PERFORMANCE

The anatomy and physiology of athletic performance are crucial for **optimizing physical performance** and **minimizing the risk of injury**. In this chapter, we will explore the key systems and processes contributing to athletic performance, including the musculoskeletal system, muscle contractions, the cardiovascular and respiratory systems, and energy production and utilization.

Unleashing the Power of Your Muscles

The musculoskeletal system is a complex and intricate system essential for movement and force transfer. It comprises bones, joints, muscles, tendons, and ligaments, which work together to allow for movement and force production.

The bones provide a framework for the body and support the muscles, while the joints allow for movement between the bones. Several types of joints, including hinge joints, ball and socket joints, and pivot joints, allow for different types of movement. The bones are also important for storing minerals, such as calcium, and for producing blood cells.

The muscles are responsible for movement and the production of force. They produce force through contraction, and there are three muscle contractions: concentric, eccentric, and isometric. Concentric contractions involve the shortening of the muscle, eccentric contractions involve the lengthening of the muscle, and isometric contractions involve the static contraction of the muscle.

The tendons and ligaments connect the muscles to the bones and provide stability. The tendons attach the muscles to the bones and transfer force. At the same time, the ligaments connect the bones and provide stability to the joints.

The musculoskeletal system is central to athletic performance, as it is responsible for movement and force production. Strong, flexible, and well-coordinated muscles are essential for optimal athletic performance, and training programs should be designed to improve these qualities. Training programs should also focus on improving the strength and flexibility of the bones, joints, tendons, and ligaments to support the musculoskeletal system and prevent injuries.

By understanding the anatomy and function of the musculoskeletal system, athletes and coaches can develop training programs tailored to improve athletic performance and reduce the risk of injury.

A Little Bit of Muscle Magic

Muscles produce force through contraction, and three muscle contractions can occur during exercise: concentric, eccentric, and isometric.

Concentric contractions occur when a muscle shortens as it contracts, such as when a bicep curls a dumbbell. During a concentric contraction, the muscle generates maximum force at its shortest length. This contraction is important for power and speed and is commonly used in jumping, throwing, and sprinting.

Eccentric contractions occur when a muscle lengthens as it contracts, such as when a bicep lowers a dumbbell back down. During an eccentric contraction, the muscle absorbs force at its longest length. This contraction can help improve muscle endurance and reduce the risk of injury, as it helps to decelerate and control movement.

Isometric contractions occur when a muscle maintains a constant length as it contracts, such as when a person holds a plank position. During an isometric contraction, the muscle generates force but does not change in length. This type of contraction is important for maintaining stability and balance, and it can also help to improve muscle strength and endurance.

Each type of muscle contraction has its unique benefits and can be trained to improve athletic performance. For example, concentric contractions are important for producing power and speed. In contrast, eccentric contractions can help improve muscle endurance and reduce the risk of injury. Finally, isometric contractions can help improve muscle strength, endurance, stability, and balance.

By understanding the different types of muscle contractions and their benefits, athletes and coaches can design training programs focusing on specific muscle contractions to improve athletic performance. For example, a sprinter may focus on training concentric contractions to improve speed. In contrast, an endurance athlete may focus on training eccentric contractions to improve muscle endurance.

It is also important to consider the balance between different types of muscle contractions in training programs. While each type of muscle contraction has its unique benefits, it is important to maintain a balance between concentric, eccentric, and isometric contractions to optimize athletic performance and prevent muscle imbalances.

Understanding how muscles produce force and the different muscle contractions during exercise is crucial for optimizing athletic performance. Athletes and coaches can design effective training programs that improve athletic performance by training specific muscle contractions and maintaining a balance between different contractions.

Cardio and Breath: The Dynamic Duo of Athletic Performance

The cardiovascular and respiratory systems play a crucial role in athletic performance. They deliver oxygen and nutrients to the muscles and remove waste products. The heart pumps oxygen-rich blood to the muscles through the circulatory system, while the lungs take in oxygen and release carbon dioxide through the respiratory system.

During exercise, the demand for oxygen and nutrients increases, and the cardiovascular and respiratory systems must work harder to deliver these essential nutrients to the muscles. As a result, the efficiency of these systems is a key factor in athletic performance, and training can improve their function and capacity.

We can train the cardiovascular system to improve efficiency through regular aerobic exercises like running, cycling, or swimming. This type of exercise helps to improve the function of the heart, lungs, and blood vessels, as well as increase the body's ability to deliver oxygen to the muscles. In addition, aerobic training can also improve the body's ability to remove waste products, such as lactic acid, from the muscles, which can help to reduce muscle fatigue.

We can also train the respiratory system to improve its efficiency through regular exercise and training techniques such as **deep breathing** and **diaphragmatic breathing**. These techniques can help improve the lungs' function and increase their capacity to take in oxygen.

In summary, the cardiovascular and respiratory systems play a crucial role in athletic performance, and training can improve their function and capacity. By training these systems through regular exercise and techniques such as deep breathing and diaphragmatic breathing, athletes and coaches can optimize athletic performance and improve the body's ability to deliver oxygen and nutrients to the muscles.

How Your Body Generates and Uses Energy During Exercise

Energy production and utilization are other important aspects of athletic performance. The body uses a combination of carbohydrates, fats, and proteins as fuel during exercise, and the type and intensity of the activity will determine which energy systems are primarily used.

The phosphagen system is the primary energy system for high-intensity, short-duration activities, such as sprinting or weightlifting.

This system uses stored ATP (adenosine triphosphate) and creatine phosphate to produce energy rapidly. Still, it can only sustain high-intensity exercise for a short period. **ATP is the primary source of energy for the body**, and it is stored in the muscles and other tissues. Creatine phosphate is also stored in the muscles and regenerates ATP during exercise.

The glycolytic system is used for moderate-intensity, moderate-duration activities like running or cycling. This system breaks down glycogen (a carbohydrate stored in the muscles) to produce energy. It can sustain moderate-intensity exercise for longer periods. However, it also produces lactic acid as a byproduct, which can lead to **muscle fatigue**. Glycogen is stored in the muscles and liver, and we can break it down into glucose, which the body uses to produce energy.

The oxidative system is used for low-intensity, long-duration activities like distance running or cycling. This system uses fat and carbohydrate stores to produce energy and sustain low-intensity exercise for extended periods. However, it is less efficient than the other energy systems and produces energy at a slower rate. The oxidative system relies on the breakdown of fats and carbohydrates to produce energy. Therefore, it is primarily used during low-intensity, long-duration exercise.

Optimizing energy production and utilization is crucial for athletic performance, and training and nutrition can play a significant role in this process. By understanding how the body produces and uses energy during exercise, athletes and coaches can develop effective training programs and nutrition plans tailored to the individual's specific needs.

For example, an athlete training for a marathon may focus on increasing their glycogen stores and improving their body's ability to use fat as fuel during long-duration exercise. On the other hand, a sprinter may focus on increasing their ATP stores and improving their body's ability to produce energy quickly and efficiently through the phosphagen system.

Understanding how the body produces and uses energy during exercise is crucial for optimizing athletic performance. By training the different energy systems and optimizing nutrition, athletes and coaches can improve the body's ability to produce and utilize energy efficiently. This can help to improve performance, reduce fatigue, and enhance recovery.

It is also important to consider the balance between different energy systems in training programs. While each energy system has unique benefits, it is important to maintain a balance between the phosphagen, glycolytic, and oxidative systems to optimize athletic performance and prevent muscle imbalances.

In this chapter, we have explored the anatomy and physiology of athletic performance and how they contribute to optimal physical performance. By understanding the musculoskeletal system, muscle contractions, the cardiovascular and respiratory systems, and energy production and utilization, athletes and coaches can develop effective training programs and nutrition plans tailored to the individual's specific needs and goals.

Chapter Summary

- The musculoskeletal system is essential for movement and force production and includes bones, joints, muscles, tendons, and ligaments.
- The bones provide a framework for the body and support the muscles, while the joints allow for movement between the bones.
- The muscles produce force through contraction, and there are three muscle contractions: concentric, eccentric, and isometric.
- Concentric contractions involve the shortening of the muscle, eccentric contractions involve the lengthening of the muscle, and isometric contractions involve the static contraction of the muscle.
- Tendons and ligaments connect the muscles to the bones and provide stability.
- Training programs should focus on improving the strength, flexibility, and coordination of the muscles and the strength and flexibility of the bones, joints, tendons, and ligaments.
- The cardiovascular and respiratory systems deliver oxygen and nutrients to the muscles during exercise.
- Energy production and utilization are important for athletic performance, as the body requires energy to perform physical activity. The body primarily uses carbohydrates and fats as fuel sources, and the balance between the two depends on the intensity and duration of the activity.

2
GENETICS AND ATHLETIC PERFORMANCE

The study of genetics involves examining how traits are inherited from one generation to the next. In the context of athletic performance, genetics plays a role in determining an individual's physical characteristics and abilities, such as **muscle structure, metabolism,** and **cardiovascular function.** While genetics is only one factor that contributes to athletic performance, it can significantly impact an athlete's potential and the sports in which they are best suited.

Inherited Genetic Traits and Athletic Ability

Inherited genetic traits can impact an individual's athletic ability in various ways. Some genetic traits linked to athletic performance include muscle fiber type, VO2 max, and muscle strength.

Muscle fiber type is a genetic trait that determines the type of muscle fibers an individual has in their body. Fast-twitch muscle fibers are responsible for short bursts of explosive power. In contrast, slow-twitch fibers are better suited for endurance activities. Individuals with a higher proportion of fast-twitch fibers may be more suited to power-based sports, such as sprinting or weightlifting. In comparison, those with a higher proportion of slow-twitch fibers may excel in endurance sports like marathon running or cycling.

VO2 max measures the body's ability to use oxygen and is often associated with endurance performance. Individuals with a high VO2 max can take in and use more oxygen during exercise, allowing them to sustain higher activity levels for longer periods. Genetics can play a role in an individual's VO2 max, with some people having a higher VO2 max than others.

Muscle strength is another genetic trait that can impact athletic performance. Strength is determined by the size and number of muscle fibers, as well as the efficiency of the nervous system in activating those fibers. Therefore, individuals with a strong genetic predisposition for muscle strength may have an advantage in sports that require strength and power, such as football or rugby.

It is important to note that while genetics can play a role in determining an individual's athletic ability, other factors, such as training, nutrition, and environment, also play a significant role in athletic performance. Therefore, by understanding the impact of inherited genetic traits on athletic ability, coaches and athletes can better tailor training programs and make informed decisions about which sports and events to pursue.

Genetic Testing for Athletic Potential

Genetic testing has become increasingly popular in recent years to predict athletic potential and tailor training programs. However, it is important to understand that **genetic testing is just one tool in the toolkit and should not be relied upon as the sole determinant of an athlete's potential.**

Genetic testing involves analyzing an individual's DNA to identify variations in specific genes that are thought to be related to athletic performance. Some common genes tested include ACTN3, which is associated with muscle fiber type, and PPARA, which is involved in fat metabolism.

While genetic testing can provide some insight into an individual's athletic potential, it is important to recognize the limitations of this type of testing. The relationship between genetics and athletic performance is complex and multifaceted, and genetic testing can only provide a partial picture. Training, nutrition, and environmental conditions also play a significant role in athletic performance. Therefore, we cannot capture them through genetic testing alone.

Additionally, the accuracy of genetic testing can vary, and the results may only sometimes be reliable. Therefore, it is important for athletes and coaches to work with qualified professionals and to interpret genetic test results in the context of other factors that may impact athletic performance.

In summary, genetic testing can provide useful information for predicting athletic potential and tailoring training programs. Still, it should not be relied upon as the sole determinant of an athlete's potential. Therefore, it is important to consider the limitations of genetic testing and to interpret the results in the context of other factors that impact athletic performance.

Tailoring Training with Genetic Information

Using genetic information to tailor training programs is a relatively new area of research in athletic performance. While genetic testing can provide some insight into an individual's athletic potential and how they may respond to different types of training, it is important to recognize this approach's limitations and consider other factors that may impact training response.

One potential use of genetic information in training is identifying an individual's muscle fiber type and tailoring training accordingly. For example, individuals with a higher proportion of fast-twitch muscle fibers may benefit from more explosive, power-based training. In comparison, those with a higher proportion of slow-twitch fibers may respond better to endurance-based training. However, it is important to note that muscle fiber type is just one factor that can impact training response. Other factors, such as training history, nutrition, and overall training load, play a role.

Another potential use of genetic information in training is identifying an **individual's risk for overtraining or injury**. For example, some genetic variations have been linked to an increased risk of overtraining or certain types of injuries. By identifying these risk factors, coaches and athletes can adjust training programs and implement strategies to prevent overtraining and injuries. However, it is important to recognize that genetics is just one factor among many that can impact the risk of overtraining or injury and that other factors, such as training load, technique, and recovery strategies, also play a role.

In summary, using genetic information to tailor training programs is a promising area of research. Still, it is important to recognize this approach's limitations and consider other factors that may impact training response. It is also important to work with qualified professionals and to interpret genetic test results in the context of an individual's overall training program.

Ethical Considerations in the Use of Genetics in Sports

The use of genetics in sports raises several ethical considerations, including discrimination, privacy, and fairness issues.

One concern is the potential for genetic discrimination in sports. If genetic testing becomes widespread, there is a risk that athletes with certain genetic traits may be unfairly excluded from certain sports or events. For example, an athlete with a genetic predisposition for muscle strength may be unfairly excluded from a weight class in a sport such as wrestling or weightlifting, even if they meet all other requirements for competition.

Another concern is the potential for the misuse of genetic information in sports. There is a risk that coaches or trainers may use genetic information to advantage certain athletes unfairly or to exclude others unfairly. This could create an uneven playing field and undermine the integrity of the competition.

There are also concerns about privacy and the potential for misusing genetic information outside sports. For example, suppose athletes undergo genetic testing as part of their training. In that case, they may risk having their genetic information accessed or used without their consent.

To address these concerns, sports organizations need to establish clear guidelines and policies for using genetic testing in sports. This could include measures to protect athletes' privacy and ensure that genetic information is not used to advantage or disadvantage athletes unfairly. It may also be necessary to establish an oversight body to monitor genetic testing in sports and ensure that it is used ethically and responsibly.

In summary, the use of genetics in sports raises several ethical considerations that must be carefully considered and addressed to ensure that the rights and interests of athletes are protected.

In conclusion, genetics plays a role in athletic performance by determining an individual's physical characteristics and abilities. Certain inherited genetic traits, such as muscle fiber type, VO2 max, and muscle strength, can impact an athlete's athletic ability and the sports in which they are best suited. As a result, genetic testing has become popular for predicting athletic potential and tailoring training programs. Still, it is important to recognize this approach's limitations and consider other factors that may impact athletic performance. In addition, genetics in sports raises several ethical considerations, including discrimination, privacy, and fairness issues. Therefore, sports organizations need to establish clear guidelines and policies for using genetic testing in sports to ensure that the rights and interests of athletes are protected. Overall, understanding genetics's role in athletic performance can help coaches and athletes make informed decisions about training and competition.

Chapter Summary

- Genetics plays a role in determining an individual's physical characteristics and abilities that impact athletic performance.
- Inherited genetic traits that can impact athletic ability include muscle fiber type, VO2 max, and muscle strength.
- Fast-twitch muscle fibers are responsible for short bursts of explosive power. In contrast, slow-twitch fibers are better suited for endurance activities.
- VO2 max measures the body's ability to use oxygen and is often associated with endurance performance.
- Strength is determined by the size and number of muscle fibers, as well as the efficiency of the nervous system in activating those fibers.
- Genetic testing involves analyzing an individual's DNA to identify variations in specific genes that are thought to be related to athletic performance.
- Genetic testing can provide useful information for predicting athletic potential and tailoring training programs. Still, it is just one tool and should not be relied upon as the sole determinant of an athlete's potential.
- Other factors, such as training, nutrition, and environment, also play a significant role in athletic performance.

3

TRAINING FOR ATHLETIC PERFORMANCE

Training is a crucial aspect of athletic performance, and understanding the principles of training and how they apply to athletic performance is essential for optimizing physical and technical performance. In this chapter, we will explore the key training principles and how we can use them to improve athletic performance.

The Principles of Training

Training involves systematically applying stress to the body to stimulate adaptation and improve physical and technical performance. Several key training principles apply to athletic performance, including overload, specificity, progression, and reversibility.

Overload is applying greater stress or demand on the body than it is accustomed to stimulating adaptation. For example, lifting progressively heavier weights or progressively running longer distances can overload the muscles and stimulate adaptation. The body will adapt to the increased demand by becoming stronger, faster, or more endurance-oriented. Applying the appropriate overload level is important, as too much can lead to overtraining and injury, while too little may not provide a sufficient stimulus for adaptation.

Specificity refers to the principle of training specifically for the demands of the sport or activity. Sports or activities have different physical and technical demands, and training should be specific to these demands to optimize performance. For example, a sprinter must train muscles to produce maximal force quickly. In contrast, distance runners must train their muscles to produce low-intensity, long-duration force.

Progression refers to gradually increasing the intensity or volume of training in a controlled and systematic manner. Progression allows the body to adapt to the increasing demands of training and avoid overtraining or injury. Therefore, it is important to progressively increase the intensity or volume of training in a controlled and logical manner rather than increasing it too quickly.

Reversibility refers to the principle that if training is stopped or significantly reduced, the adaptations gained from training will begin to decline. Therefore, maintaining a consistent training program is essential for maintaining the adaptations gained from training. For example, suppose athletes take a significant break from training. In that case, they may lose some of the strength, endurance, or other physical qualities they gained through training. This is why it is important to maintain a consistent training program to maintain the adaptations gained from training.

In summary, the principles of training are important for optimizing athletic performance. By understanding and applying the principles of overload, specificity, progression, and reversibility, athletes and coaches can develop effective training programs tailored to the individual athlete's specific needs and goals. These principles help ensure that training is effective, efficient, and safe and can help athletes reach their full potential and succeed in their sport.

The Benefits of Periodization and Variety in Training

Periodization is the systematic planning and organization of training over some time. It involves dividing the training year into blocks or phases, each with a specific focus or goal. Periodization allows athletes to vary their training and avoid overtraining or boredom. In addition, it can help athletes peak for important competitions or events.

Several types of training can be used as part of a periodized training program, including endurance, strength, power, speed, skill development, and recovery.

Endurance training involves training the body's ability to sustain prolonged physical activity. It is important for sports that involve long-distance or sustained effort, such as running, cycling, or swimming. Endurance training can improve the efficiency of the cardiovascular and respiratory systems, as well as the muscles' ability to use oxygen and produce energy.

Strength training involves using resistance exercises to improve muscle size, strength, and power. In addition, strength training can improve athletic performance by increasing the force production capabilities of the muscles and improving bone density and joint stability.

Power training involves exercises that produce maximum force in the shortest time, such as plyometrics or Olympic lifts. Power training can improve explosive power and speed, which can be important for sports that require quick bursts of force, such as basketball, soccer, or football.

Speed training involves exercises focusing on improving movement speed, such as sprinting or agility drills. Speed training can improve athletic performance by increasing movement speed and the body's ability to change direction quickly.

Skill development involves practicing and refining specific technical skills, such as throwing, hitting, or shooting. Skill development is crucial for sports that require specific technical skills, and we can improve it through deliberate practice and repetition.

Recovery is an important aspect of training, as it allows the body to repair and adapt to training demands. Recovery can include rest, massage, or active recovery exercises, which are important for maintaining optimal performance and reducing the risk of injury.

In conclusion, periodization is a crucial aspect of training that helps athletes and coaches organize and structure training to optimize performance and avoid overtraining. By dividing the training year into blocks or phases with specific goals and focuses, athletes can vary their training and peak for important competitions or events. Several types of training can be used as part of a periodized training program, including endurance, strength, power, speed, skill development, and recovery. By understanding the different types of training and how we can use them in a periodized program, athletes and coaches can develop effective training programs tailored to the individual athlete's specific needs and goals.

The Role of Strength Training in Athletic Performance

Strength training is a type of training that involves the use of resistance exercises to improve muscle size, strength, and power. Strength training can be an important aspect of athletic performance, as it can improve the muscles' force production capabilities and bone density, and joint stability.

Several strength training exercises can improve athletic performance, including free weights, machines, and bodyweight exercises. Free weights, such as dumbbells, barbells, and kettlebells, allow for a greater range of movement and can be more effective for improving functional strength. Machines, such as weight machines or cable machines, provide a more controlled movement and can be useful for targeting specific muscle groups. Finally, bodyweight exercises, such as push-ups, squats, and lunges, use the body's weight as resistance and can improve functional strength.

The intensity, volume, and frequency of strength training should be carefully planned and progressively increased to allow for optimal adaptation and avoid overtraining or injury. Strength training should be specific to the needs and goals of the individual, and it should be integrated into a well-rounded training program that includes other types of training, such as endurance, power, and skill development.

In conclusion, strength training is an important aspect of athletic performance that can improve the muscles' force production capabilities, bone density, and joint stability. Several strength training exercises can improve athletic performance, including free weights, machines, and bodyweight exercises. The intensity, volume, and frequency of strength training should be carefully planned and progressively increased to allow for optimal adaptation and avoid overtraining or injury. Strength training should be specific to the needs and goals of the individual, and it should be integrated into a well-rounded training program that includes other types of training, such as endurance, power, and skill development. By understanding the role of strength training in athletic performance and how to incorporate it into a training program effectively, athletes and coaches can optimize athletic performance and reach their full potential.

Skill Development and Technique in Athletic Performance

Athletic performance heavily depends on the technical skills required by the sport or activity. Whether it's throwing a ball with precision, hitting it with power, or shooting it with accuracy, the ability to execute these skills with proper technique is essential for success. This is why skill development and technique are so important in athletic performance.

Deliberate practice is a key component of skill development. This involves focusing on specific skills or techniques and practicing them to improve. **Repetition** is also important, as it allows the body to ingrain the proper movement patterns and muscle memory needed for proper technique. Coaches and trainers can help athletes develop skills through various methods, including verbal cues, demonstrations, and feedback.

The technique is another important aspect of athletic performance. Proper technique can help improve the efficiency and effectiveness of a skill, as well as reduce the risk of injury. Coaches and trainers can help athletes refine their technique through verbal cues, demonstrations, and feedback. We can also use technology to track and improve techniques, such as video analysis or wearable sensors.

In conclusion, skill development and technique are essential for optimal athletic performance. Deliberate practice and repetition are key components of skill development. Proper technique can improve efficiency and reduce the risk of injury. Coaches and trainers are crucial in helping athletes develop and refine their skills and technique. Technology can also be a useful tool in this process.

This chapter has explored the key training principles and how they apply to athletic performance. We have discussed the importance of periodization in training and the different types of training that can be used to optimize performance, including endurance, strength, power, speed, skill development, and recovery. We have also examined the role of strength training in athletic performance and the importance of skill development and technique in optimizing technical performance. By understanding the principles of training and how they apply to athletic performance, athletes and coaches can develop effective training programs tailored to the individual's specific needs and goals. In the coming chapters, we will delve deeper into the role of nutrition in athletic performance and how it can be optimized to support training and performance.

Chapter Summary

- Training involves applying stress to the body to stimulate adaptation and improve physical and technical performance.
- Key training principles include overload, specificity, progression, and reversibility.
- Overload involves applying greater stress or demand on the body than it is accustomed to.
- Specificity involves training specifically for the demands of the sport or activity.
- Progression involves gradually increasing the intensity or volume of training in a controlled and systematic manner.
- Reversibility refers to the principle that if training is stopped or significantly reduced, the adaptations gained from training will begin to decline.
- Periodization is the systematic planning and organization of training over time. It involves dividing the training year into blocks or phases with specific focuses or goals.
- Several types of training can be used in a periodized training program, including endurance, strength, power, speed, skill development, and recovery.

4

NUTRITION AND ATHLETIC PERFORMANCE

Proper nutrition is essential for optimal athletic performance, as it supports the body's ability to recover from training, repair and build new tissues, and produce energy. In this chapter, we will explore the role of nutrition in athletic performance and how it can be optimized to support training and performance.

The Role of Nutrition in Athletic Performance

Nutrition is a complex and multifaceted aspect of athletic performance. Athletes need to understand the specific nutritional needs of their sport and their bodies to optimize their performance. This includes understanding the role of different macronutrients, such as carbohydrates, proteins, and fats, as well as the importance of micronutrients, such as vitamins and minerals.

Carbohydrates are the body's primary energy source during exercise and should be most athletes' primary fuel source. Carbohydrates can be found in various foods, such as grains, fruits, and vegetables. We should consume them appropriately based on the intensity and duration of the activity.

Protein is important for building and repairing tissues. Therefore, it is especially important for athletes who engage in high-intensity or strength-based training. Good protein sources include meat, poultry, fish, beans, and dairy products.

Fats are also an important energy source for the body and are necessary for maintaining healthy skin, hair, and joints. Fats can be found in foods such as nuts, seeds, and avocados, and we should consume them in appropriate amounts.

Micronutrients, such as vitamins and minerals, are essential for maintaining good health and optimal athletic performance. They can be found in various foods, such as fruits, vegetables, and fortified foods. Therefore, we should consume them appropriately to meet the body's needs.

Proper nutrition is essential for athletic performance. Therefore, athletes should work with a registered dietitian or sports nutritionist to develop a nutrition plan that meets their specific needs and goals.

The Importance of Proper Hydration and Electrolyte Balance

Proper hydration is essential for athletic performance. It supports the body's ability to regulate temperature, transport nutrients and oxygen, and remove waste products. Dehydration can significantly impact athletic performance, leading to fatigue, muscle cramps, and impaired mental function.

Athletes should **aim to drink enough fluids to replace any fluids lost through sweat during exercise** and drink before, during, and after exercise to maintain hydration. Water is the primary fluid needed for hydration. Still, athletes may also need to replace electrolytes, such as sodium and potassium, lost through sweat. Sports drinks and electrolyte supplements can replace electrolytes during prolonged or intense exercise.

The Role of Macronutrients in Athletic Performance

Macronutrients are nutrients that the body needs in large amounts and include carbohydrates, proteins, and fats. Each macronutrient plays a unique role in athletic performance and can be important for optimizing energy production, repair and recovery, and body composition.

Carbohydrates are the body's primary energy source and are important for athletic performance, particularly high-intensity or endurance activities. Carbohydrates can be stored in the muscles and liver as glycogen, which we can break down to produce energy during exercise. Therefore, consuming adequate amounts of carbohydrates before, during, and after exercise can help maintain glycogen stores and support energy production.

Proteins are important for building and repairing tissues, such as muscles. They are also involved in the production of enzymes and hormones. Therefore, adequate protein intake is important for athletic performance, as it can support muscle repair, growth, and immune function.

Fats are an important source of energy and are also important for hormone production and cell membrane structure. Fats can be used as an energy source during exercise, particularly during low-intensity or endurance activities. However, excess intake of fats can lead to weight gain and negatively impact athletic performance.

The specific macronutrient needs of athletes depend on the demands of the sport, the intensity and duration of the training, and the individual's goals. Therefore, athletes should work with a sports dietitian or nutritionist to determine their specific macronutrient needs and how they can be met through a balanced diet and supplements, if necessary.

Micronutrients (Vitamins and Minerals) in Athletic Performance

Micronutrients are nutrients that the body needs in small amounts, including vitamins and minerals. These nutrients play important roles in various physiological processes and can be important for athletic performance.

Vitamins are essential for the proper functioning the body's systems and can be important for athletic performance. For example, vitamin C is important for immune function, and vitamin D is important for bone health. Vitamin E is an antioxidant that can help protect cells from oxidative stress caused by intense exercise. Vitamin K is important for blood clotting and bone health.

Minerals are essential for various physiological processes, such as electrolyte balance and muscle contraction. Therefore, mineral deficiencies can negatively impact athletic performance. Therefore, if necessary, athletes must consume adequate minerals through a balanced diet or supplements. Some important minerals for athletic performance include calcium, which is important for bone health, and sodium and potassium, which help regulate electrolyte balance and muscle contractions. Iron is also important for oxygen transport to the muscles, and a deficiency can lead to fatigue and impaired performance.

Athletes must consume a varied and balanced diet that includes adequate micronutrients and macronutrients such as carbohydrates, proteins, and fats. Individual needs may vary based on the type and intensity of the sport, as well as the athlete's age, gender, and training status. Working with a sports dietitian can help athletes determine their specific nutrient needs and develop a personalized nutrition plan.

In summary, micronutrients are important for various physiological processes that support athletic performance. Therefore, adequate intake of micronutrients through a varied and balanced diet or supplements can help optimize performance and reduce the risk of deficiencies or health problems. If necessary, athletes must pay attention to their micronutrient intake and work with a sports dietitian to ensure optimal nutrition.

In this chapter, we have explored the role of nutrition in athletic performance and how it can be optimized to support training and performance. We have discussed the importance of proper hydration, electrolyte balance, and macronutrients, such as carbohydrates, proteins, and fats, in athletic performance. We have also examined the role of micronutrients, such as vitamins and minerals, in athletic performance. By understanding the role of nutrition in athletic performance, athletes and coaches can develop effective nutrition plans tailored to the individual's specific needs and goals.

Chapter Summary

- Proper nutrition is essential for optimal athletic performance. It supports the body's ability to recover from training, repair and build new tissues, and produce energy.
- Macronutrients, such as carbohydrates, proteins, and fats, are nutrients that the body needs in large amounts and play unique roles in athletic performance.
- Carbohydrates are the body's primary energy source and are important for high-intensity or endurance activities.
- Proteins are important for building and repairing tissues and are involved in the production of enzymes and hormones.
- Fats are an important source of energy and are also important for hormone production and cell membrane structure.
- Micronutrients, such as vitamins and minerals, are essential for maintaining good health and optimal athletic performance.
- Proper hydration is essential for athletic performance. It supports the body's ability to regulate temperature, transport nutrients and oxygen, and remove waste products.
- Athletes should aim to drink enough fluids to replace any fluids lost through sweat during exercise and drink before, during, and after exercise to maintain hydration. They may also need to replace electrolytes lost through sweat.

5

PERFORMANCE-ENHANCING SUBSTANCES AND DOPING

Performance-enhancing substances, also known as **performance-enhancing drugs** (PEDs), are substances that are taken to improve athletic performance. These include legal and illegal substances, such as anabolic steroids, stimulants, and hormone supplements. PEDs, also known as doping, is a controversial topic in sports. They can give athletes an unfair advantage and undermine the integrity of the competition. While some athletes may use PEDs to gain a competitive edge, using these substances can have serious risks and consequences, including increased risk of injury, long-term health problems, and even death in some cases. As a result, PEDs are strictly prohibited in many sports and are subject to strict penalties and sanctions. To protect the health and well-being of athletes and maintain the integrity of competition, sports organizations have implemented various methods for detecting and preventing doping, including testing programs and education initiatives.

Types of Performance-Enhancing Substances

Performance-enhancing substances, or performance-enhancing drugs (PEDs), are substances that are taken to improve athletic performance.

Many different types of PEDs can have a range of effects on athletic performance. Some common types of PEDs include:

Anabolic steroids: Anabolic steroids are synthetic hormones that mimic the effects of testosterone in the body. Athletes often use these substances to increase muscle mass, strength, and endurance. However, anabolic steroids can have serious side effects, including liver damage, heart problems, and hormonal imbalances.

Stimulants: Stimulants are substances that increase energy levels and alertness. Common stimulants used as PEDs include caffeine, amphetamines, and ephedrine. These substances can have various side effects, including increased heart rate, hypertension, and insomnia.

Hormone supplements: Hormone supplements, such as human growth hormone (HGH) and erythropoietin (EPO), increase muscle mass and endurance. HGH is a hormone that is naturally produced by the body. At the same time, EPO is a hormone that stimulates the production of red blood cells. Hormone supplements can have serious side effects, including an increased risk of cancer, heart problems, and kidney damage.

Diuretics: Diuretics are substances that increase urine production, which can help reduce weight and increase muscle definition. However, diuretics can also cause dehydration, electrolyte imbalances, and other health problems.

Masking agents: Masking agents are substances used to prevent the detection of other PEDs in drug testing. These substances can include substances that interfere with drug testing procedures or that are used for flushing PEDs out of the body. Masking agents are strictly prohibited in many sports and can result in significant penalties and sanctions.

In summary, many different types of performance-enhancing substances can have a range of effects on athletic performance. Therefore, athletes need to be aware of the risks and consequences of using PEDs and the strict penalties and sanctions we can impose for doping. In addition to the physical risks associated with PED use, athletes caught using these substances may face significant legal and professional consequences, including disqualification from the competition, loss of sponsorships, and damage to their reputation. Therefore, it is important for athletes to understand the risks and consequences of using PEDs and to make informed decisions about whether to use these substances.

Risks and Consequences of Using Performance-Enhancing Substances

Performance-enhancing substances, or performance-enhancing drugs (PEDs), can have a range of risks and consequences for athletes. Some of the potential risks and consequences of using PEDs include the following:

Physical risks: PEDs can have a range of physical risks and side effects, depending on the specific substance and the method of use. Some common risks associated with PED use include liver damage, heart problems, hormonal imbalances, and an increased risk of injury. In some cases, the use of PEDs can even be fatal.

Legal consequences: PEDs are strictly prohibited in many sports and are subject to strict penalties and sanctions. Athletes caught using PEDs may face disqualification from the competition, loss of titles and awards, and fines. In some cases, using PEDs may also be illegal and can result in criminal charges.

Professional consequences: PEDs can have significant professional consequences for athletes, including loss of sponsorships, damage to their reputation, and difficulty finding future sports opportunities. In addition to the financial implications of these consequences, the loss of professional opportunities can be emotionally and mentally challenging for athletes.

Ethical implications: Using PEDs raises several ethical concerns, including issues related to fairness and the integrity of the competition. Athletes who use PEDs may be seen as cheating and undermining the trust of their peers, fans, and the wider community.

Psychological consequences: PEDs can have psychological consequences for athletes, including increased pressure to perform, guilt, and shame. Athletes caught using PEDs may also face social ostracism and struggle to rebuild their reputation and credibility.

In summary, using PEDs can have serious risks and consequences for athletes, including physical, legal, professional, ethical, and psychological implications. Therefore, it is important for athletes to be aware of these risks and consequences and to make informed decisions about whether to use PEDs.

Methods of Detecting and Preventing Doping in Sports

To maintain the integrity of competition and protect the health and well-being of athletes, sports organizations have implemented various methods for detecting and preventing doping in sports. Some common methods for detecting and preventing doping include:

Drug testing: Drug testing is a commonly used method for detecting the use of performance-enhancing substances in sports. Drug testing can be conducted through urine, blood, or other types of samples and detect the presence of a wide range of PEDs. Independent agencies typically conduct drug testing. It follows strict protocols to ensure the accuracy and reliability of the results.

Education and awareness programs: Many sports organizations and governing bodies have implemented education and awareness programs to educate athletes about the risks and consequences of doping and to promote fair play. These programs can include information about the types of PEDs prohibited, the risks and consequences of using these substances, and the methods used to detect and prevent doping.

Therapeutic Use Exemptions (TUEs): In some cases, athletes may have a legitimate medical need for a substance that is otherwise prohibited in their sport. In these cases, athletes can apply for a Therapeutic Use Exemption (TUE) to use the substance for therapeutic purposes. TUEs are granted a case-by-case basis and require strict documentation and oversight to prevent abuse.

In-competition and out-of-competition testing: Many sports organizations conduct both in-competition and out-of-competition testing to detect the use of PEDs. In-competition testing occurs during actual competition and is designed to detect the use of PEDs that may have a performance-enhancing effect during the event. Out-of-competition testing occurs outside competition and is designed to detect the use of PEDs that may have a long-term performance-enhancing effect or to identify doping patterns. Out-of-competition testing allows sports organizations to test athletes more frequently and can deter doping more effectively.

Biological Passport: The Biological Passport is a program that uses long-term monitoring of an athlete's biological markers to detect the use of PEDs. The Biological Passport involves collecting and analyzing multiple athletes' samples over time to create a profile of their normal levels of certain markers. If the levels of these markers deviate from the athlete's normal profile, it may indicate PED use. The Biological Passport is used in conjunction with traditional drug testing. It is considered to be a more effective deterrent to doping.

In summary, various methods are used to detect and prevent doping in sports, including drug testing, education and awareness programs, Therapeutic Use Exemptions (TUEs), in-competition and out-of-competition testing, and the Biological Passport. These methods are designed to protect athletes' health and well-being and maintain the integrity of competition in sports.

Ethical Considerations in the Use of Performance-Enhancing Substances in Sports

The use of performance-enhancing substances, or performance-enhancing drugs (PEDs), in sports raises several ethical considerations. Some of the ethical issues related to the use of PEDs in sports include the following:

Fairness: PEDs can give athletes an unfair advantage over their competitors, undermining the fairness of competition. This can be particularly problematic in individual sports, where one athlete's performance can directly affect the event's outcome. Using PEDs can also create uncertainty in competition, as it is difficult to know whether an athlete's performance is the result of natural ability or the use of PEDs.

Health risks: Using PEDs can have serious health risks for athletes, including long-term health problems and even death in some cases. Using PEDs can also create an unhealthy culture in sports, where athletes feel pressured to take risks with their health to succeed.

Professional integrity: Using PEDs can damage athletes' professional integrity and undermine the trust of fans, sponsors, and the wider community. Athletes caught using PEDs may face significant consequences, including loss of titles, awards, and sponsorships and damage to their reputation.

Legal implications: The use of PEDs can have legal implications for athletes, as the possession, use, and distribution of certain PEDs may be illegal in some jurisdictions. Athletes caught using PEDs may face criminal charges in addition to the sanctions imposed by their sport.

Personal autonomy: Using PEDs raises questions about personal autonomy and the right of athletes to make their own decisions about their bodies and careers. Some may argue that athletes should have the freedom to decide whether to use PEDs. In contrast, others may argue that the risks and consequences of PED use are too great and that athletes should be protected from making potentially harmful decisions. This complex ethical issue requires balancing the rights of athletes to make their own decisions with the need to protect the health and well-being of athletes and the integrity of the competition.

In conclusion, using performance-enhancing substances in sports raises several ethical considerations, including fairness, health risks, professional integrity, legal implications, and personal autonomy. Therefore, it is important for athletes, coaches, and sports organizations to consider these ethical issues when making decisions about using PEDs and to strive for fair and ethical practices in sports.

This chapter explored the performance-enhancing substances used in sports, including anabolic steroids, stimulants, hormone supplements, diuretics, and masking agents. We also examined the risks and consequences of using these substances, including the physical risks, legal and professional consequences, and ethical considerations. Finally, we discussed the methods used to detect and prevent doping in sports, including drug testing, education and awareness programs, Therapeutic Use Exemptions (TUEs), in-competition and out-of-competition testing, and the Biological Passport.

It is important for athletes, coaches, and sports organizations to be aware of the risks and consequences of using PEDs and to strive for fair and ethical practices in sports. By understanding the impact of PEDs on athletic performance and the methods used to detect and prevent doping, we can work towards a more fair and ethical sports culture.

Chapter Summary

- Performance-enhancing substances, also known as performance-enhancing drugs (PEDs), are substances taken to improve athletic performance.
- PEDs include legal and illegal substances, such as anabolic steroids, stimulants, hormone supplements, diuretics, and masking agents.
- PEDs can give athletes an unfair advantage and undermine the integrity of competition.
- PEDs can have serious risks and consequences, including increased risk of injury, long-term health problems, and even death in some cases.
- PEDs are strictly prohibited in many sports and are subject to strict penalties and sanctions.
- Sports organizations have implemented methods for detecting and preventing doping, including testing programs and education initiatives.
- Risks and consequences of using PEDs include physical risks, legal and professional consequences, and ethical considerations.
- To ensure fair competition and protect the health and well-being of athletes, it is important for athletes to understand the risks and consequences of using PEDs and to make informed decisions about whether to use these substances.

6
PSYCHOLOGICAL FACTORS IN ATHLETIC PERFORMANCE

Psychological factors can significantly impact athletic performance, and understanding their role and how to optimize them can be crucial for optimal performance. This chapter will explore the psychological factors affecting athletic performance and how we can manage them to improve performance.

The Role of Psychological Factors in Athletic Performance

Psychological factors, such as **motivation, confidence, focus, stress,** and **anxiety**, can significantly impact athletic performance. These factors can affect an athlete's ability to perform to their full potential. Both internal and external factors can influence them.

Motivation is an important psychological factor affecting athletic performance, as it drives an athlete's desire and determination to succeed. Motivation can be influenced by various factors, including personal goals, feedback from coaches and teammates, and the desire to succeed.

Confidence is another important psychological factor that can impact athletic performance. Confidence is an athlete's belief in their ability to succeed. It can be influenced by past performance, support from others, and training and preparation.

Focus is the ability to concentrate and direct attention, which is important for athletic performance, particularly in sports requiring mental focus and decision-making. Conversely, distractions or lack of focus can negatively impact performance, and techniques such as visualization or pre-performance routines can help athletes maintain focus.

Stress and **anxiety** can also affect athletic performance, as they can interfere with an athlete's ability to perform to their full potential. Stress and anxiety can be caused by various internal and external factors, such as pressure to perform, fear of failure, or physical or mental fatigue.

Stress and Anxiety in Athletic Performance and How to Manage Them

The role of stress and anxiety in athletic performance is complex, as both can have positive and negative effects on an athlete's performance. On the one hand, a certain stress level can act as a motivator, helping athletes focus and perform at their best. However, on the other hand, if stress and anxiety reach unmanageable levels, they can become detrimental to performance.

Stress and anxiety can impact athletic performance by interfering with an athlete's ability to concentrate, focus, and make decisions. This can be particularly problematic in sports that require split-second decisions or quick reactions. Chronic stress and anxiety can also lead to physical and mental fatigue, negatively impacting performance.

There are several strategies that athletes can use to manage stress and anxiety and improve performance. One effective technique is **relaxation training,** which can include *deep breathing, progressive muscle relaxation,* or *meditation.* These techniques help athletes relax and focus their attention, which can benefit performance. In addition, mental skills training, such as goal setting or visualization, can help manage stress and anxiety.

Suppose an athlete is struggling with stress and anxiety. In that case, they need support from a coach, sports psychologist, or mental health professional. These individuals can help athletes develop healthy coping strategies and manage stress and anxiety. It is also important for athletes to maintain a healthy lifestyle, including getting enough sleep, eating a balanced diet, and engaging in regular physical activity. This can help athletes manage their stress and anxiety levels and improve their overall performance.

Mental Skills Training in Athletic Performance

Mental skills training can be particularly useful for athletes competing in high-pressure situations, such as championship games or close contests. In these situations, mental skills training can help athletes maintain their focus and concentration and prevent distractions from affecting their performance.

Mental skills training can also be helpful for athletes who are recovering from injury or facing setbacks in their careers. By developing mental skills such as goal setting and positive self-talk, athletes can stay motivated and focused on their long-term goals, even during difficult times.

Athletes need to be proactive in their mental skills training, as it can take time to develop and refine these skills. Athletes should be committed to practicing and refining their mental skills regularly. They should be open to seeking guidance and support from coaches, sports psychologists, or other mental skills professionals. Athletes can improve their overall performance and achieve their full potential in their sport by investing in their mental skills training.

In this chapter, we have explored the psychological factors affecting athletic performance and how we can manage them to optimize performance. We have discussed the importance of motivation, confidence, and focus in athletic performance, the role of stress and anxiety, and how to manage them. We have also examined the importance of mental skills training in athletic performance and how we can incorporate it into an athlete's training program. By understanding the psychological factors that can impact athletic performance and how to optimize them, athletes and coaches can develop strategies to improve mental performance and manage stress and anxiety. In the next chapter, we will explore the role of genetics in athletic performance and how it can impact an athlete's potential and development.

Chapter Summary

- Psychological factors, such as motivation, confidence, focus, stress, and anxiety, can significantly impact athletic performance.
- Stress and anxiety can interfere with an athlete's ability to concentrate, focus, and make decisions.
- Relaxation techniques, such as deep breathing, progressive muscle relaxation, and meditation, can help athletes manage stress and anxiety and improve performance.
- Mental skills training, including goal setting and visualization, can help athletes manage stress and anxiety and improve performance.
- Athletes need to seek support from a coach, sports psychologist, or mental health professional if they struggle with stress and anxiety.
- Maintaining a healthy lifestyle, including getting enough sleep, eating a balanced diet, and engaging in regular physical activity, can help athletes manage stress and anxiety and improve overall performance.
- Team cohesion, or unity and cooperation within a team, can also impact athletic performance.
- Techniques such as communication skills training and team bonding activities can help improve team cohesion and enhance performance.

7

RECOVERY AND INJURY PREVENTION IN ATHLETIC PERFORMANCE

Recovery and injury prevention are crucial for optimal athletic performance, as they support the body's ability to adapt and improve from training. They also reduce the risk of injury. This chapter will explore the importance of recovery and injury prevention in athletic performance and discuss strategies for optimizing recovery and preventing injuries.

Recovery and Injury Prevention in Athletic Performance

Recovery and injury prevention are essential aspects of athletic performance, as they allow the body to repair and adapt to the demands of training and competition. Proper recovery and injury prevention strategies can help athletes maintain optimal performance, reduce the risk of injury, and prevent overtraining.

Athletes can use several recovery methods to support their bodies and optimize performance, including **active recovery, passive recovery, nutrition,** and **sleep**. Active recovery involves low-intensity activities such as light stretching or yoga, which can help the body recover and improve flexibility. Passive recovery methods, such as massage or ice baths, can help reduce inflammation and muscle soreness. Adequate nutrition and hydration are also important for recovery, as they provide the body with the necessary nutrients and fluids to repair and rebuild tissues. Finally, sleep is crucial for recovery, as it allows the body to repair and regenerate tissues and replenish energy stores.

Injury prevention is also important in athletic performance, as **injuries can significantly impact an athlete's ability to train and compete.** There are several strategies that athletes can use to prevent injuries, including warm-up and cool-down routines, proper technique, and the use of protective equipment. Proper technique is particularly important, as poor technique can increase the risk of injury. Athletes should also be aware of their bodies, listen to any warning signs of potential injuries, such as pain or discomfort, and seek medical attention if necessary.

In summary, recovery and injury prevention is essential for optimal athletic performance. By understanding the different types of recovery methods and strategies for injury prevention, athletes and coaches can develop effective training programs that support the body and reduce the risk of injury.

The Different Types of Recovery Methods and Their Effectiveness

Recovery and injury prevention are crucial for optimal athletic performance, as they allow the body to repair and rebuild tissues that have been damaged during training, as well as reduce the risk of injury. In addition, proper recovery and injury prevention strategies can help athletes maintain a consistent training program, which is essential for maintaining the adaptations gained from training.

Athletes can use several recovery methods to optimize recovery and prevent injuries, including active recovery, passive recovery, nutrition, and sleep. Active recovery involves low-intensity exercise or movement that helps to flush out waste products and improve circulation, such as walking or light stretching. Passive recovery involves rest, such as massage or cold water immersion. It can be effective in reducing muscle soreness and inflammation.

Proper nutrition is also crucial for recovery, providing the body with the necessary nutrients for repairing and rebuilding tissues. Adequate intake of carbohydrates, proteins, and fluids can help support recovery and reduce muscle soreness. Adequate sleep is also important for recovery, allowing the body to repair and rebuild tissues and support immune function. Lack of sleep can negatively impact athletic performance and increase the risk of injury.

Injury prevention is also an important aspect of athletic performance, and there are several strategies that athletes can use to reduce the risk of injury. These strategies include proper warm-up and cool-down techniques, using proper technique and form during training, and using appropriate equipment and protective gear. In addition, strength training and flexibility training can also help to improve muscle balance and reduce the risk of injury.

It is important for athletes to find a balance between recovery and training and to incorporate a variety of recovery methods into their training program. By prioritizing recovery and injury prevention, athletes can optimize their performance and reduce the risk of setbacks.

Common Athletic Injuries and Strategies for Preventing Them

Athletic injuries are common and can significantly impact athletic performance. Common athletic injuries include muscle strains, sprains, and stress fractures.

We can use several strategies to prevent athletic injuries, including proper training and conditioning, warm-up and cool-down, and proper technique and form. Wearing appropriate protective equipment, such as helmets or mouthguards, can also help reduce the risk of injury.

Proper training and conditioning can help reduce the risk of injury by building strength and flexibility and gradually increasing the intensity and duration of training. Proper warm-up and cool-down routines can also help reduce the risk of injury by preparing the body for exercise and helping to reduce muscle soreness and fatigue.

Proper technique and form are important for preventing injuries, particularly in sports that involve specific technical skills. Coaches and trainers can play a crucial role in teaching proper technique and form and providing feedback to athletes to help them improve their technique.

In addition to these strategies, **athletes must listen to their bodies** and recognize when they are feeling tired or experiencing pain. Overuse injuries, such as tendonitis or stress fractures, can often be prevented by taking breaks and allowing the body to rest and recover. Regular stretching and foam rolling can also help reduce the risk of injury by improving flexibility and mobility.

Proper nutrition and hydration are also important for injury prevention. They can support the body's immune system and help maintain optimal physical function. In addition, adequate intake of nutrients, such as protein, carbohydrates, and electrolytes, can help support muscle repair and recovery. In contrast, proper hydration can help maintain optimal muscle function and prevent cramping.

Finally, athletes need to **seek medical attention** if they experience an injury. Early diagnosis and treatment can help prevent the injury from worsening and speed up recovery. Physical therapists and athletic trainers can also be valuable resources for helping athletes recover from injuries and preventing future injuries.

In this chapter, we have explored the importance of recovery and injury prevention in athletic performance and discussed strategies for optimizing recovery and preventing injuries. We have examined the different recovery methods and their effectiveness and discussed common athletic injuries and prevention strategies. By understanding the importance of recovery and injury prevention and how to optimize them, athletes and coaches can develop effective strategies to maintain physical and mental well-being and optimize performance.

Chapter Summary

- Recovery and injury prevention is essential for optimal athletic performance, as they allow the body to repair and adapt to the demands of training and competition.
- Recovery methods include active recovery (low-intensity exercise or movement), passive recovery (rest), nutrition, and sleep.
- Proper nutrition is important for recovery, providing the body with the necessary nutrients for repairing and rebuilding tissues.
- Adequate sleep is also crucial for recovery, allowing the body to repair and rebuild tissues and support immune function.
- Strategies for injury prevention include proper warm-up and cool-down techniques, proper technique and form during training, and appropriate equipment and protective gear.
- Strength and flexibility training can also help prevent injuries by improving muscle strength and balance.
- Working with a coach or sports medicine professional can help athletes develop an effective recovery and injury prevention plan.
- Athletes need to listen to their bodies and seek medical attention to prevent injuries from worsening.

8
TECHNOLOGY AND ATHLETIC PERFORMANCE

Technology has significantly impacted athletic performance and how athletes train and compete. In this chapter, we will explore the role of technology in athletic performance and discuss the use of wearable technology, data analysis, and performance modeling, as well as the potential future developments in technology and their impact on athletic performance.

The Role of Technology in Athletic Performance

Technology has played an increasingly significant role in athletic performance in recent years. From wearable sensors to video analysis software, technology can provide athletes with valuable insights and data that can help them optimize their training and performance.

One of the primary ways that technology has impacted athletic performance is through **wearable sensors**, such as fitness trackers or GPS watches. These devices can give athletes real-time data on their physical activity, including heart rate, distance traveled, and burned calories. We can use this information to monitor training intensity, track progress, and adjust training programs.

Video analysis software is another technology that has significantly impacted athletic performance. This software allows athletes and coaches to review and analyze video footage of training sessions or competitions to identify strengths, weaknesses, and areas for improvement. Video analysis can be particularly useful for sports that involve specific technical skills, such as throwing, hitting, or shooting, as it can provide insights into an athlete's technique and form.

Technology has also impacted how coaches and trainers communicate and interact with athletes. For example, apps and software can provide a platform for coaches to share training programs, schedules, and other important information with athletes and facilitate communication and feedback.

Overall, technology has had a significant impact on athletic performance, and it is likely to continue to play a major role in the future. By leveraging the power of technology, athletes and coaches can gain valuable insights and data that can help optimize training and performance.

Wearable Technology in Training and Competition

Wearable technology, such as fitness trackers, smartwatches, and GPS devices, have become increasingly popular in recent years and have been adopted by many athletes for training and competition purposes. Wearable technology can provide athletes with valuable data and insights that can help improve their performance and track their progress.

One common use of wearable technology in training is to track and monitor physical activity. Wearable devices can track various metrics, such as heart rate, steps taken, distance traveled, and calories burned, which can help athletes monitor their training intensity and volume. Wearable devices can also provide feedback on technique, such as stride length and cadence, which can help athletes optimize their training and improve their performance.

In competition, athletes can use **wearable technology to monitor performance and track progress in real-time**. For example, GPS devices can provide athletes with speed, distance, and pacing data, which can help them optimize their performance and make strategic decisions during a race. Wearable devices can also give athletes real-time feedback on their technique, such as swing speed or stroke rate, which can help them make adjustments and improve their performance.

Wearable technology can also be used to **monitor recovery and prevent injuries**. For example, wearable devices can track sleep quality and heart rate variability, providing valuable insights into an athlete's recovery status. Wearable devices can also alert if an athlete is at risk of overtraining or needing a break to recover.

Overall, wearable technology has the potential to significantly improve athletic performance by providing athletes with valuable data and insights that can help them optimize their training, track their progress, and monitor their recovery. However, it is important for athletes to carefully consider the types of wearable technology most suitable for their needs and use them responsibly and thoughtfully.

Data Analysis and Performance Modeling in Athletic Performance

The use of data analysis and performance modeling has become increasingly prevalent in the world of athletics as coaches and athletes seek to gain a competitive edge through the use of data-driven approaches. Data analysis involves collecting and interpreting data to inform decision-making and performance. We can use it in various ways to improve athletic performance.

One way data analysis can be used in athletics is by **tracking physical performance data**, such as speed, power, and endurance. Wearable technology, such as GPS tracking devices and heart rate monitors, can collect this data and provide insights into an athlete's physical capabilities and training needs. By analyzing this data, coaches and athletes can identify areas of strength and weakness and develop targeted training programs to improve performance.

Performance modeling is another way data analysis can be used in athletics. Performance modeling involves using mathematical models and algorithms to predict an athlete's future performance based on past performance data. This can be useful for predicting the outcomes of competitions and developing training programs tailored to an athlete's specific needs and goals.

Data analysis and performance modeling can also **inform tactical decision-making in team sports**. By analyzing data on an opponent's strengths and weaknesses, coaches can develop strategies that exploit their own team's strengths and exploit their opponent's weaknesses. Data analysis can also be used to inform the player selection and substitution decisions, as well as to identify areas of the game where the team needs to improve.

Overall, athletic data analysis and performance modeling can provide valuable insights and help coaches and athletes make informed decisions about training and competition. As a result, athletes and coaches can optimize performance and gain a competitive edge by leveraging data and technology.

Potential Future Developments in Technology

There are several potential future developments in technology that could impact athletic performance in the coming years. One of these developments is using **artificial intelligence (AI) and machine learning in sports analytics and performance modeling**. AI and machine learning algorithms can analyze large amounts of data, such as athlete performance data, to identify patterns and trends that we can use to optimize training and performance.

Another potential future technological development is **virtual reality (VR) and augmented reality** (AR) in training and competition. We can use VR and AR to simulate real-world environments and scenarios, allowing athletes to train in a more realistic and immersive environment. VR and AR can also be used to improve coaching and analysis, as they can provide a more accurate and detailed view of an athlete's performance.

Wearable technology is also expected to continue to evolve and improve, potentially developing more advanced sensors and devices that can track and analyze a wider range of physiological and performance data. These devices could provide athletes with real-time feedback and guidance, helping them optimize their performance.

Another potential future technological development is using **biometric sensors and smart clothing**. Biometric sensors can track and analyze various physiological parameters, such as heart rate and body temperature, and smart clothing can incorporate these sensors into garments that we can wear during training and competition. This technology could provide athletes with more accurate and detailed data about their body's responses to exercise, allowing them to optimize their training and performance.

Overall, future technological developments are expected to significantly impact athletic performance in the coming years, providing athletes with new tools and technologies to optimize their training and performance. Therefore, it is important for athletes and coaches to stay up-to-date with these developments and to consider how we can use them to enhance performance.

In this chapter, we have explored the role of technology in athletic performance and discussed the use of wearable technology, data analysis, and performance modeling. We have also examined the potential future technological developments and their impact on athletic performance. By understanding the role of technology in athletic performance and the potential future developments, athletes and coaches can develop strategies to optimize performance and training.

Chapter Summary

- Technology has had a significant impact on athletic performance, including the use of wearable sensors, data analysis software, and performance modeling.
- Wearable technology, such as fitness trackers and GPS watches, can provide athletes with data on their physical activity, including heart rate and distance traveled, to optimize training intensity and track progress.
- Video analysis software allows athletes and coaches to review and analyze video footage of training sessions and competitions to identify areas for improvement.
- Apps and software can provide a platform for coaches to communicate with athletes and share training programs and schedules.
- Athletes can also use wearable technology in competition to monitor performance and track progress in real-time.
- Wearable devices can track sleep quality and heart rate variability to monitor recovery and prevent injuries.
- Data analysis and performance modeling can help athletes and coaches identify trends and predict future performance.
- Future developments in technology, such as virtual reality and biometric sensors, have the potential to impact athletic performance further.

9

ENVIRONMENTAL FACTORS IN ATHLETIC PERFORMANCE

Several factors influence athletic performance, including genetics, training, nutrition, and psychology. In addition to these internal factors, external environmental conditions can significantly impact athletic performance. Environmental conditions such as altitude, temperature, humidity, and wind can affect an athlete's physical abilities. They can have a direct impact on the outcome of a sporting event. This chapter will explore how environmental conditions impact athletic performance and how athletes can prepare for and adapt to these conditions.

Altitude and Athletic Performance

Altitude is a key environmental factor that can impact athletic performance. Altitude refers to the height above sea level at which an athlete is training or competing. At higher altitudes, the air is thinner and contains less oxygen, which can affect an athlete's physical abilities.

The impact of altitude on athletic performance is due to the physiological changes in the body when exposed to a lower oxygen environment. The body must work harder to obtain oxygen at higher altitudes, leading to increased heart rate, ventilation, and blood flow. These physiological changes can affect an athlete's physical abilities, including endurance, strength, and power.

The effects of altitude on athletic performance can vary depending on the individual athlete and the specific sport. Some athletes may be more affected by altitude than others, and certain sports may be more impacted by altitude than others. For example, endurance sports, such as running, cycling, and triathlon, may be more affected by altitudes than power sports, such as football or basketball.

There are several strategies that athletes can use to prepare for and adapt to the effects of altitude. One approach is to **train at a high altitude for some time before competing at altitude.** This can help the body adapt to the lower oxygen environment and improve athletic performance. Other strategies include using **oxygen supplements** or **sleeping in hypoxic tents**, which simulate high altitude conditions.

Altitude is a key environmental factor that can impact athletic performance. The physiological changes in the body at high altitudes can affect an athlete's physical abilities, and the impact of altitude can vary depending on the athlete and the specific sport. Therefore, athletes can optimize their performance at altitude by understanding the effects of altitude and using strategies to prepare for and adapt to high altitude conditions.

Temperature and Athletic Performance

Temperature is another environmental factor that can impact athletic performance. The body's internal temperature must be regulated to maintain optimal physical and mental function. When the body becomes too hot or cold, it can affect an athlete's physical abilities and performance.

Generally, the **optimal temperature for athletic performance** is around **68-72 degrees Fahrenheit (20-22 degrees Celsius)**. However, the body may overheat at temperatures above this range, leading to increased heart rate, sweating, and fatigue. This can affect an athlete's endurance, strength, and power and may increase the risk of heat-related illness.

On the other hand, the body may begin to cool down at temperatures below this range, leading to decreased heart rate, blood flow, and muscle function. This can affect an athlete's physical abilities and increase the risk of injury. Cold temperatures can also affect an athlete's mental function and focus, making it more difficult to perform at their best.

There are several strategies that athletes can use to prepare for and adapt to different temperature conditions. For example, athletes can stay hydrated in hot temperatures, wear lightweight and breathable clothing, and seek shade or use cooling devices to help regulate their body temperature. In cold temperatures, athletes can wear layers of clothing, use hand and foot warmers, and perform dynamic stretches to help keep their muscles warm and flexible.

In summary, the temperature is an important environmental factor that can impact athletic performance. By understanding the effects of temperature on the body and using strategies to prepare for and adapt to different temperature conditions, athletes can optimize their performance and reduce the risk of heat-related illness or injury.

Humidity and Athletic Performance

Humidity, or the amount of moisture in the air, is another environmental factor that can impact athletic performance. High humidity levels can affect an athlete's physical abilities and performance by making it more difficult for the body to regulate its internal temperature.

When the air is humid, sweat does not evaporate from the skin as easily, making it harder for the body to cool down. This can lead to increased heart rate, sweating, and fatigue, affecting an athlete's endurance, strength, and power. High humidity levels can also make breathing more difficult, affecting an athlete's cardiovascular function and performance.

On the other hand, low humidity levels can lead to dehydration and decreased sweating, affecting an athlete's ability to regulate their body temperature and increasing the risk of heat-related illness.

There are several strategies that athletes can use to prepare for and adapt to different humidity levels. For example, athletes can stay hydrated in high-humidity conditions, wear lightweight and breathable clothing, and use cooling devices to help regulate their body temperature. In low-humidity conditions, athletes can drink electrolyte-rich fluids and use moisturizing products to prevent dry skin.

In summary, humidity is an important environmental factor impacting athletic performance. By understanding the effects of humidity on the body and using strategies to prepare for and adapt to different humidity levels, athletes can optimize their performance and reduce the risk of heat-related illness or dehydration.

Wind and Athletic Performance

The wind is another environmental factor that can impact athletic performance. Wind can affect an athlete's physical abilities and performance in several ways, depending on the strength and direction of the wind and the specific sport being played.

For example, in sports that involve throwing or hitting a ball, such as a baseball, golf, or tennis, wind can affect the trajectory and distance of the ball. In addition, wind can affect an athlete's speed and energy expenditure in running and cycling, with headwinds making it more difficult to move forward and tailwinds providing a boost. In outdoor sports, wind can also affect an athlete's balance and stability, making it more difficult to maintain control.

There are several strategies that athletes can use to prepare for and adapt to wind conditions. For example, in sports that involve throwing or hitting a ball, athletes can practice in windy conditions to develop the skills and techniques needed to compensate for wind. In running and cycling, athletes can adjust their pace and strategy based on the wind direction and strength. Finally, athletes can use crouching or a lower center of gravity in outdoor sports to maintain balance and stability in windy conditions.

In summary, the wind is an environmental factor that can impact athletic performance in various sports. By understanding the effects of wind on physical abilities and performance and using strategies to prepare for and adapt to wind conditions, athletes can optimize their performance and maintain control in windy conditions.

Weather Conditions and Athletic Performance

Weather conditions, such as temperature, humidity, and wind, can all impact athletic performance. In addition to these factors, other types of weather, such as **rain**, **snow**, and **lightning**, can also affect athletic performance.

Rain can affect an athlete's grip and traction, as well as their visibility and concentration. In sports involving running, jumping, or throwing, rain can make the field or surface slippery, increasing the risk of injury and affecting an athlete's physical abilities. In sports that involve handling a ball or equipment, rain can make the ball or equipment wet and slippery, affecting an athlete's grip and control.

Snow can affect an athlete's traction and stability, as well as their visibility and concentration. In sports involving running, jumping, or throwing, snow can make the field or surface slippery, increasing the risk of injury and affecting an athlete's physical abilities. In sports that involve handling a ball or equipment, snow can make the ball or equipment cold and hard, affecting an athlete's grip and control.

Lightning poses a significant safety risk to athletes, especially in outdoor sports. When lightning is present, athletes must seek shelter and avoid playing or practicing until the storm has passed.

There are several strategies that athletes can use to prepare for and adapt to different weather conditions. For example, athletes can wear appropriate footwear and clothing in rainy or snowy conditions to improve traction and stability. In sports that involve handling a ball or equipment, athletes can use strategies such as using a different grip or adjusting the way they throw or hit the ball to compensate for wet or slippery conditions. In the event of lightning, athletes should follow established protocols for seeking shelter and avoiding play or practice until the storm has passed.

In summary, weather conditions, including temperature, humidity, wind, rain, snow, and lightning, can all impact athletic performance. By understanding the effects of different weather conditions on physical abilities and performance and using strategies to prepare for and adapt to different weather conditions, athletes can optimize their performance and reduce the risk of injury.

This chapter has explored how environmental factors, such as altitude, temperature, humidity, wind, and weather conditions, can impact athletic performance. These factors can affect an athlete's physical abilities and performance, depending on the sport played and the specific environmental conditions.

Altitude, for example, can affect an athlete's oxygen uptake and cardiovascular function. At the same time, temperature and humidity can impact their ability to regulate their body temperature and stay hydrated. In addition, wind can affect an athlete's speed and trajectory. In contrast, weather conditions like rain, snow, and lightning can affect an athlete's traction, stability, and visibility.

By understanding the impact of environmental factors on athletic performance and using strategies to prepare for and adapt to different conditions, athletes can optimize their performance and reduce the risk of injury. Athletes, coaches, and sports organizations need to be aware of how environmental factors can impact athletic performance and take steps to mitigate their impact.

Chapter Summary

- Environmental conditions such as altitude, temperature, humidity, and wind can impact athletic performance.
- Altitude affects athletic performance due to physiological changes in the body caused by thinner air with less oxygen at higher altitudes. These changes can affect endurance, strength, and power.
- Athletes can prepare for and adapt to high altitude conditions by training at high altitudes beforehand or using oxygen supplements or hypoxic tents.
- The optimal temperature for athletic performance is around 68-72 degrees Fahrenheit (20-22 degrees Celsius). Higher temperatures can lead to increased heart rate, sweating, and fatigue. In comparison, lower temperatures can lead to decreased heart rate, blood flow, and muscle function.
- Humidity can impact athletic performance by affecting the body's ability to regulate its temperature through sweating. High humidity makes sweat harder to evaporate and cool the body, leading to increased heat stress and fatigue.
- Wind can affect athletic performance by increasing the effort required to move through it, particularly in sports such as running and cycling. Wind can also affect the trajectory and movement of objects in sports such as golf, baseball, and tennis.
- To prepare for and adapt to different environmental conditions, athletes can use strategies such as staying hydrated, wearing appropriate clothing, using cooling or warming devices, and performing dynamic stretches.

EPILOGUE

This book explores the science behind athletic performance and the various factors that can impact athletic performance. We have examined the anatomy and physiology of athletic performance and how the musculoskeletal, cardiovascular, and respiratory systems contribute to athletic performance. We have also discussed training principles and the importance of periodization, strength training, and skill development in athletic performance.

We have explored the role of nutrition in athletic performance, the importance of proper hydration and electrolyte balance, and the role of macronutrients and micronutrients in athletic performance. We have also examined the psychological factors that can impact athletic performance, such as motivation, confidence, focus, stress, and anxiety, and how we can manage them to optimize performance.

We have discussed the importance of recovery and injury prevention in athletic performance and the various methods and strategies we can use to optimize recovery and prevent injuries. We have also examined the role of technology in athletic performance and the use of wearable technology, data analysis, and performance modeling.

In conclusion, understanding the science behind athletic performance is crucial for optimizing training and performance. By understanding the various factors impacting athletic performance and how we can manage them, athletes and coaches can develop strategies to optimize training and performance.

AFTERWORD

As you come to the end of "*The Athlete's Blueprint to Success*," we hope you have gained a comprehensive understanding of the many factors that contribute to athletic success. From developing winning habits and managing finances to understanding the science of athletic performance, this guidebook has provided you with the tools you need to reach your full potential.

We hope that you have found the information in this book to be insightful and valuable. Whether you are an athlete or a coach, remember that success in athletics is a journey, not a destination. By consistently applying the principles and strategies outlined in this book, you can continue to optimize your physical and mental performance and achieve your goals.

We wish you all the best in your athletic pursuits. We are confident that "*The Athlete's Blueprint to Success*" will be a valuable resource on your journey. Thank you for choosing this book; we hope to hear about your successes in the future.

ABOUT THE AUTHOR

Hadley Mannings is a seasoned athlete and coach with a decade of experience in the field. He has a deep-rooted passion for helping others reach their maximum potential and has spent countless hours studying the science behind athletic success. In *"The Athlete's Blueprint to Success,"* he provides a comprehensive guidebook that encompasses his extensive knowledge of the multifaceted factors that contribute to athletic performance, including anatomy and physiology, training principles, nutrition, and mental skills training. In his leisure time, he can be found pushing his limits by participating in triathlons and imparting his wisdom to the next generation of athletes as a track and field coach.

~~$10.99~~ FREE EBOOK

Receive Your Free Copy of Legends of the Game

Or visit:
bookboundstudios.wixsite.com/hadley-mannings

www.ingramcontent.com/pod-product-compliance
Lightning Source LLC
Chambersburg PA
CBHW072046110526
44590CB00018B/3062